Contents

1 Introduction

1.1 Did you know? **1**

1.2 What's in a name? **2**

1.3 Registering births in England and Wales **3**

1.4 Interest in names **4**

2 The top 100 names in England and Wales between 1944 and 1994

2.1 Introduction **6**

2.2 Top 10 girls' names at ten year intervals **7**
Commentary **7**
Table A: Top 10 girls' names, 1944-1994, England and Wales **8**

2.3 Top 10 boys' names at ten year intervals **9**
Commentary **9**
Table B: Top 10 boys' names, 1944-1994, England and Wales **9**

2.4 Ranking and frequency: girls' names 1-100 **10**
Commentary and overview **10**
Table 1: Top 100 girls' names, 1944-1994, England and Wales **12**

2.5 Ranking and frequency: boys' names 1-100 **20**
Commentary and overview **20**
Table 2: Top 100 boys' names, 1944-1994, England and Wales **22**

2.6 Ranking and number: girls' names A-Z **28**

Commentary and overview **28**
Table 3: Alphabetical Top 100 girls' names, 1944-1994, England and Wales **30**

2.7 Ranking and number: boys' names A- Z **36**
Commentary and overview **36**
Table 4: Alphabetical Top 100 boys' names, 1944-1994, England and Wales **38**

3 The top 50 names in the Regions in 1994

3.1 Introduction **44**

3.2 Regional overview – Girls **46**

3.3 Girls' names in the North **48**
Commentary **48**
Table 5: Top 50 girls' names, 1994, North **49**

3.4 Girls' names in Yorkshire and Humberside **50**
Commentary **50**
Table 6: Top 50 girls' names, 1994, Yorkshire and Humberside **51**

3.5 Girls' names in the East Midlands **52**
Commentary **52**
Table 7: Top 50 girls' names, 1994, East Midlands **53**

3.6 Girls' names in East Anglia **54**
Commentary **54**
Table 8: Top 50 girls' names, 1994, East Anglia **55**

3.7 Girls' names in the South East including Greater London **56**
Commentary **56**
Table 9: Top 50 girls' names, 1994, South East including Greater London **57**

3.8 Girls' names in Greater London **58**
Commentary **58**
Table 10: Top 50 girls' names, 1994, Greater London **59**

3.9   Girls' names in the South East excluding Greater London **60**
Commentary **60**
Table 11: Top 50 girls' names, 1994, South East excluding
Greater London **61**

3.10 Girls' names in the South West **62**
Commentary **62**
Table 12: Top 50 girls' names, 1994, South West **63**

3.11 Girls' names in the West Midlands **64**
Commentary **64**
Table 13: Top 50 girls' names, 1994, West Midlands **65**

3.12 Girls' names in the North West **66**
Commentary **66**
Table 14: Top 50 girls' names, 1994, North West **67**

3.13 Girls' names in Wales **68**
Commentary **68**
Table 15: Top 50 girls' names, 1994, Wales **69**

3.14 Regional overview – Boys **70**

3.15 Boys' names in the North **72**
Commentary **72**
Table 16: Top 50 boys' names, 1994, North **73**

3.16 Boys' names in Yorkshire and Humberside **74**
Commentary **74**
Table 17: Top 50 boys' names, 1994, Yorkshire and Humberside **75**

3.17 Boys' names in the East Midlands **76**
Commentary **76**
Table 18: Top 50 boys' names, 1994, East Midlands **77**

3.18 Boys' names in East Anglia **78**
Commentary **78**
Table 19: Top 50 boys' names, 1994, East Anglia **79**

3.19 Boys' names in the South East including Greater London **80**
Commentary **80**
Table 20: Top 50 boys' names, 1994, South East including Greater London **81**

3.20 Boys' names in Greater London **82**
Commentary **82**
Table 21: Top 50 boys' names, 1994, Greater London **83**

3.21 Boys' names in the South East excluding Greater London **84**
Commentary **84**
Table 22: Top 50 boys' names, 1994, South East excluding Greater London **85**

3.22 Boys' names in the South West **86**
Commentary **86**
Table 23: Top 50 boys' names, 1994, South West **87**

3.23 Boys' names in the West Midlands **88**
Commentary **88**
Table 24: Top 50 boys' names, 1994, West Midlands **89**

3.24 Boys' names in the North West **90**
Commentary **90**
Table 25: Top 50 boys' names, 1994, North West **91**

3.25 Boys' names in Wales **92**
Commentary **92**
Table 26: Top 50 boys' names, 1994, Wales **93**

4   Further Information

4.1   Birth, Death and Marriage Certificate Services from the GRO **94**

Appendix A

How the lists were compiled **96**
Table C: NHS Registrations by sex and year of birth **97**
Table D: NHS Registrations by sex, births in 1994, Standard Regions **97**

1

Introduction

1.1 Did you know?

Did you know...

- that 1 in 12 baby boys born in 1944 were named John?
- that the most popular girls name in 1954, Susan, was given to twice as many babies as the next most popular – Linda or Christine?
- that Heather is one of only seven girls' names to have remained in the Top 100 names given to baby girls throughout the period 1944–1994?
- that Gareth is only to be found in the Wales Top 50?
- that Alice is much more popular in the south than the north, accounting for 1 in 67 baby girls in the South West, but only 1 in 160 in the North?
- that, as a rule, 100 baby girls are born for every 105–106 baby boys?

What were the other most popular names in the last 50 years? How have they changed? What are the differences across the country? This book provides you with much of the information that will help you monitor the changes and look in more detail at the names recently given to babies across the country. It contains information about the 100 most popular first names of babies born in 1944, 1954, 1964, 1974, 1984 and 1994, and about the 50 most popular first names of babies born in 1994 in each of the regions.

The names that are listed are the first forenames only. Variant spellings of the same name such as Stephen and Steven have been treated as separate names.

The information is based on some three quarters of a million babies' names in 1944 and 1954, over a million in 1964, one of the baby boom years, and around 700,000 in the years 1974, 1984, 1994.

1.2 What's in a name?

You need your full name nowadays, particularly for official purposes such as getting married, obtaining a driving licence or passport or proving a claim to an inheritance. But in the past people would have used personal names only. Surnames were introduced following the Norman conquest and used to group people according to their clan or family, or type of work, and thus distinguish between those with the same forename. Later still they came to indicate class distinctions. The regional, occupational and class implications of surnames are well documented.

'"Good afternoon", I managed to say.
"How do you do?" she said. "Mr Cohen?"
"Er-no."
"Mr Fred Stone?"
"Not absolutely. As a matter of fact, my name's Wooster – Bertie Wooster."
She seemed disappointed. The fame of the name of Wooster seemed to mean nothing in her life.'
The Aunt and the Sluggard, P.G. Wodehouse

'"If you ever have occasion to write to me, would you mind sticking on P at the beginning of my name? P-S-M-I-T-H see? There are too many Smiths, and I don't care for Smythe... I shall start a new dynasty."'
Mike and Psmith, P.G. Wodehouse

But what about first names in recent years? Was the Essex girl of the 1980s really called Sharon or Tracy? Are there any Hooray Henries in the North? Is John still a popular name?

Some parents like to be imaginative when naming their offspring. This practice has a long history. The modern practice of naming children after football teams finds a precedent in the laundryman Arthur Pepper who, in 1882, gave his daughter a forename beginning with each letter of the alphabet except P. In 1886 an uneducated general labourer Robert Restell named his son *That's it, who'd have thought it.* It is not known whether the recipient of this unusual name changed it when he came of age. One who did not was the son of Thomas Day, whimsically named *Time of,* who was still listed under this name at the birth of his daughter

Edna Mary in 1927. Modern examples of such parental eccentricity account for too small a proportion of births to appear in this book, but the parent seeking to avoid widely popular names will find these listings invaluable.

1.3 Registering births in England and Wales

In 1837 the Registration Act introduced the national civil registration of births, marriages and deaths to be administered by the General Register Office (GRO, now part of OPCS). New registers were begun from this time.

Indexes to the registers are kept in the Public Search Room at St. Catherine's House, London, and are used to obtain copies of certificates. They are used by people for official purposes and researching their family history. Every day around 1600 people visit the Public Search Room. Some 290,000 birth certificates were issued either to visitors or by post in the past year.

When a baby's birth is registered, the registrar gives it an NHS number at the same time, and sends these details to OPCS who add them to the National Health Service Central Register (NHSCR). It is from this register that the information in this book has been compiled. If you want to know more about the methods used to compile these listings, please see Appendix A.

Notes
See Muriel Nissel's *People Count* (OPCS, 1987) for more information on the history of registration in England and Wales.

See Certificate Services on page 94 for more information on ordering certificates.

See *Population Trends*, No 62, Winter 1990 (OPCS, 1990) for more information on the information on the work of the NHSCR.

1.4 Interest in names

Since the *Times* newspaper began to publish their annual listing of the most popular names appearing in their birth announcements column in the previous year (January, 1948 onwards), OPCS has frequently been asked for information on the population as a whole. *First Names* is designed to meet this demand.

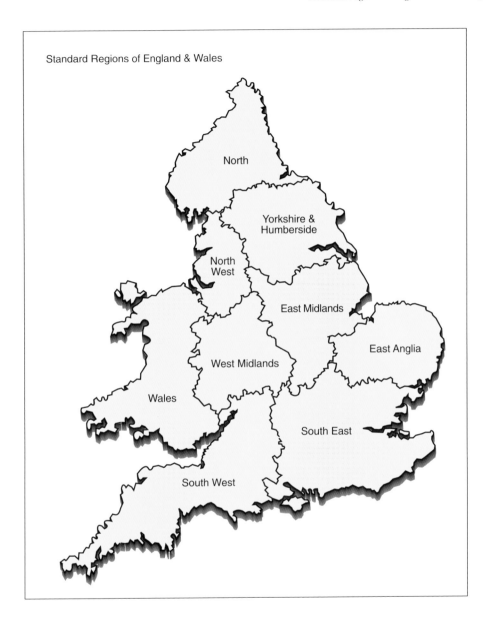

Standard Regions of England & Wales

2

The Top 100 names

England and Wales between 1944 and 1994

2.1 Introduction

Did you know...

- that 7 boys' names in the 1994 Top 10 were not there in 1984?
- that 28 boys' names appear in the Top 100 in each of the selected years from 1944–1994?
- that in 1994 the top 5 names accounted for one quarter of all baby boys?
- that Margaret was No 1 in 1944, but no longer appeared in the Top 100 in 1964?
- that girls' names seem to endure for 30 years maximum in the Top 10?
- that only 233 births separated the top 2 girls' names in 1994?

What were the other 95 boys' names in 1994? What were the 28 consistently popular names given to baby boys since 1944?

The answers to these and similar queries can be found in the following group of tables. They list the names in various ways to provide information on the changes in rank, frequencies or numbers of particular names.

The top 10 girls' and boys' names at 10 year intervals from 1944 to 1994 appear in Tables A and B. They enable the reader to see at a glance the names predominant in the selected year. These can then be explored further using Tables 1–4 where the name's rank, frequency and number are given.

The top 100 names in each of the years 1994, 1984, 1974, 1964, 1954 and 1944 are shown separately for girls and boys in Tables 1 and 2. The first column begins with the 1994 names in order of rank from 1st to 100th. These names are cross-referenced across the years. Next to appear in the first column are the 1984 names which do not occur in 1994. Again these are listed in rank order and cross-referenced. 1974 names follow, and so on to the 1944 names. The ranking (the numbers in the green columns) of each name in each year in which it appears in the Top 100 is given to enable relative positions to be traced. Frequencies are given to make it easier to make comparisons with other years.

The names are reordered alphabetically in Tables 3 and 4 with their rank and number of occurrences. Those readers interested in the number of occurrences may find it interesting that the top girls' and boys' names have each been given to over 20,000 babies in 1964, almost double the second most popular name.

Parental choice of girls' and boys' names has changed over 50 years. Why have some names suddenly increased or decreased in popularity whilst others have continued to be given by parents? Have some been influenced by the names of entertainers in music, film, theatre and TV dramas, or perhaps by football and other sporting heroes of the time?

This book does not set out to give explanations of these trends, but readers may find it interesting to speculate over possible associations with personalities that were popular at the time. For example, were parents more influenced by the names of film stars in the 1940s and 1950s, actresses such as Audrey Hepburn, Diana Dors, Susan Hayward and Marilyn Monroe? Was there any connection between the start of Emma's popularity in the seventies with the character Emma Peel in the TV series The Avengers? Have the names of characters in soap operas been chosen by parents in recent years?

You can chart the course of a particular name over the years, first by using Table 3 or 4, the alphabetical Top 100s, to obtain the ranking and year of exit from the Top 100. You will then find it in the left hand column of Table 1 or 2 as appropriate and be able to scan across the green ranking columns to trace its course.

2.2 Top 10 girls' names at ten year intervals

Commentary
The Top 10 girls' names at 10 years' intervals from 1944 to 1994 are shown in Table A. Jean, Ann, Maureen and Barbara appear only in the 1944 list. Pole

position was taken by Susan in both 1954 and 1964 from 7 in 1944. Christine was at number 3 in both 1954 and 1944. Margaret dropped from 1 in 1944 to4 in 1954.

New entries in 1954 were Linda, Carol, Elizabeth and Anne. Elizabeth may have been brought to the fore once again by the newly-crowned Queen Elizabeth II.

Only Susan remained in the 1964 Top 10. Among the new entries in that list were Helen and Karen, which in turn were the only names from the 1964 list to appear in the 1974 list.

Table A – Top 10 girls' names, 1944–1994, England and Wales

	1994	1984	1974	1964	1954	1944
1	Rebecca	Sarah	Sarah	Susan	Susan	Margaret
2	Lauren	Laura	Claire	Julie	Linda	Patricia
3	Jessica	Gemma	Nicola	Karen	Christine	Christine
4	Charlotte	Emma	Emma	Jacqueline	Margaret	Mary
5	Hannah	Rebecca	Lisa	Deborah	Janet	Jean
6	Sophie	Claire	Joanne	Tracey	Patricia	Ann
7	Amy	Victoria	Michelle	Jane	Carol	Susan
8	Emily	Samantha	Helen	Helen	Elizabeth	Janet
9	Laura	Rachel	Samantha	Diane	Mary	Maureen
10	Emma	Amy	Karen	Sharon	Anne	Barbara

In 1974 Sarah emerged at the top, a position held onto in 1984. Karen plummeted to 10 from 3. Seven names were new. One of them was Emma, a name that has continued to rise in popularity.

Emma, Claire, Samantha and Sarah kept their rankings in 1984. All the other names were new entries.

In 1994 Emma seemed to be declining in popularity, falling from its 4th position to 10th. Laura was also in decline. Amy was making steady upwards progress. And Rebecca rose to the number 1 spot.

2.3. Top 10 boys' names at ten year intervals

Commentary

The Top 10 boys' names at ten year intervals from 1944 to 1994 are shown in Table B. As with the girls' names, there is no name that appears in all years. However in general boys' names do seem to be more enduring than girls' names.

Anthony, Brian and William do not appear after 1944, their places usurped by Richard, Paul and Robert. John and David reversed the top 2 positions from 1944 to 1954.

In 1964 David retained its top position, but John dropped to 5 from 2. Paul rose from 7 to 2. Falling slightly were Michael, Stephen and Robert. Richard remained at 10. Creeping into the top ten was Ian. Andrew and Mark were the other new entries displacing Christopher, Peter and Alan.

Table B – Top 10 boys' names, 1944–1994, England and Wales

	1994	1984	1974	1964	1954	1944
1	Thomas	Christopher	Paul	David	David	John
2	James	James	Mark	Paul	John	David
3	Jack	David	David	Andrew	Stephen	Michael
4	Daniel	Daniel	Andrew	Mark	Michael	Peter
5	Matthew	Michael	Richard	John	Peter	Robert
6	Ryan	Matthew	Christopher	Michael	Robert	Anthony
7	Joshua	Andrew	James	Stephen	Paul	Brian
8	Luke	Richard	Simon	Ian	Alan	Alan
9	Samuel	Paul	Michael	Robert	Christopher	William
10	Jordan	Mark	Matthew	Richard	Richard	James

Paul finally made it to number 1 in 1974. Richard suddenly rose from 10 to 5. After 30 years away, James reappeared. Christopher returned after just 20 years in the wilderness. Simon and Matthew were new entries.

In 1984 only Simon disappeared from the list to be replaced by Daniel. James and Christopher rose to the top of the list, displacing Paul and Mark.

1994 showed a dramatic turn away from the recent stock of standard names in favour of new entries, many of which have been well-used traditionally: Thomas, Jack, Ryan, Joshua, Luke, Samuel and Jordan.

2.4. Ranking and frequency: girls' names 1–100

Commentary and overview

Parents choose from a large pool of girls' names. Whereas there are 245 girls' names that have ever appeared in the Top 100 in any of the selected years, there are 49 fewer boys' names. A favoured stock of girls' names as there is for boys is becoming an increasingly remote prospect. How English and Welsh parents would protest if presented with the equivalent of the French prescribed list of names! Even now, when French parents go to register their baby at the town or city hall, it is at the discretion of the officials to decide whether they may depart from the names of the saints in the Catholic calendar.

Only the following names appear in all years: Sarah, Elizabeth, Jennifer, Catherine, Heather, Helen and Maria.

New entries in 1994 were Bethany, Megan, Olivia, Georgia, Shannon, Paige, Nicole, Chelsea, Grace, Molly, Amber, Jasmine, Kayleigh, Harriet, Ashleigh, Francesca, Abbie, Rosie, Aimee, Lydia, Hollie, Bethan, Amelia, Beth, Ella, Robyn, Chantelle, Ellen, Daisy, Demi, Courtney, Gabrielle, Yasmin, Lily, Rhiannon, Imogen, Rebekah, Jordan and Caitlin.

On their way up are Rebecca, Lauren, Jessica, Charlotte, Hannah, Sophie, Amy, Emily, Chloe, Lucy, Jade, Alice, Danielle, Holly, Abigail, Stephanie, Natasha, Eleanor, Georgina, Gemma, Kirsty, Alexandra, Melissa, Jodie, Leah, Naomi, Aimee and Sian.

On their way down are Laura, Emma, Sarah, Katie, Rachel, Samantha, Elizabeth, Victoria, Zoe, Natalie, Jennifer, Hayley, Louise, Katherine, Anna, Kelly, Catherine, Nicola, Kate, Claire, Leanne, Rachael, Kimberley, Stacey, Kathryn, Heather, Lisa, Helen, Maria, Kerry, Joanna, Jemma and Toni.

In decline after 1944 are Beryl, Betty, Bridget, Cynthia, Daphne, Doris, Evelyn, Glenys, Gloria, Gwendoline, Iris, Lilian, Marjorie, Marlene, Mavis, Monica, Muriel, Norma, Phyllis, Vera and Vivienne.

25 names are pushed out after 1954: Audrey, Brenda, Christina, Diana, Doreen, Dorothy, Eileen, Geraldine, Glynis, Hazel, Hilary, Irene, Jean, Joan, Josephine, Joy, Joyce, June, Marian, Marilyn, Marion, Penelope, Rita, Sylvia and Veronica.

Out of favour after the swinging sixties' are Annette, Barbara, Carole, Carolyn, Frances, Gail, Janet, Janice, Jeanette, Jill, Judith, Kathleen, Kay, Lynda, Lyn, Lynne, Mandy, Margaret, Maureen, Maxine, Michele, Pamela, Pauline, Rosemary, Sheila, Shirley, Theresa, Valerie and Yvonne.

Seventies names include Anita, Ann, Anne, Beverley, Carol, Clair, Debbie, Debra, Denise, Diane, Elaine, Gillian, Heidi, Jayne, Julia, Lesley, Linda, Lorraine, Nichola, Patricia, Paula, Sandra, Sharon, Sonia, Tara, Teresa, Tina, Tracy, Vanessa, Wendy.

Girls who will come of age in the first decade of the twenty-first century are Alison, Amanda, Andrea, Angela, Carla, Carly, Caroline, Charlene, Cheryl, Christine, Clare, Dawn, Deborah, Donna, Fiona, Jacqueline, Jane, Jenna, Jenny, Joanne, Gale, Karen, Katy, Kim, Lindsay, Lindsey, Lyndsey, Lynsey, Marie, Mary, Melanie, Michelle, Ruth, Sally, Sara, Susan, Suzanne, Tanya and Tracey.

Table 1

Top 100 girls' names,

1944–1994, England and Wales

Example: Rebecca is 1st in 1994, given to 1 in 40 babies in that year. But if you look at the 1984 columns you will see that it was 5th in that year, given to 1 in 45 babies. If you want to know when it entered the Top 100, scan across the other columns. You will see that the 1944 and 1954 columns are blank. So you know Rebecca appeared for the first time in the Top 100 in 1964.

	1994		1984		1974		1964		1954		1944	
	Rank	1 in	Rank	1 in	Rank	1 in	Rank	1 in	Rank	1 in	Rank	1 in
Rebecca	1	40	5	45	16	91	98	504				
Lauren	2	41	33	164								
Jessica	3	43	40	179								
Charlotte	4	45	22	99	41	186						
Hannah	5	45	20	91	67	359						
Sophie	6	47	38	177	85	460			x	x	x	x
Amy	7	53	10	64								
Emily	8	57	36	171	80	430						
Laura	9	61	2	34	54	246	97	501				
Emma	10	61	4	40	4	43						
Chloe	11	72	97	571								
Sarah	12	76	1	29	1	26	13	74	68	310	86	534
Lucy	13	81	24	104	38	172						
Katie	14	84	13	70	81	434						
Bethany	15	88										
Jade	16	90	73	387								
Megan	17	90										
Alice	18	98	83	468								
Rachel	19	107	9	63	12	69	74	306				
Samantha	20	110	8	60	9	66						
Danielle	21	113	27	143								
Holly	22	129	59	305								
Abigail	23	131	80	439								
Olivia	24	136										
Stephanie	25	138	31	160	61	308	100	517	96	551		

	1994		1984		1974		1964		1954		1944	
	Rank	in	Rank	in	Rank	in	Rank	in	Rank	in	Rank	in
Elizabeth	26	143	25	121	23	114	20	92	8	61	15	60
Victoria	27	148	7	58	18	95						
Natasha	28	149	47	212	55	271						
Georgia	29	150										
Zoe	30	150	41	181	30	138						
Natalie	31	151	16	72	48	215						
Eleanor	32	153	76	411								
Shannon	33	167										
Paige	34	169										
Georgina	35	170	84	470	79	429					84	527
Gemma	36	173	3	39								
Nicole	37	178										
Chelsea	38	181										
Kirsty	39	182	42	182	62	308						
Alexandra	40	184	52	270	82	436						
Melissa	41	201	62	327								
Jennifer	42	214	11	67	34	147	45	162	23	109	18	66
Hayley	43	216	19	89	53	244						
Louise	44	221	17	77	13	72	47	179				
Katherine	45	221	29	156	43	198	76	334				
Jodie	46	225	53	276								
Grace	47	235										
Anna	48	242	39	177	40	186	81	367	88	505		
Molly	49	246										
Amber	50	248										
Jasmine	51	252										
Kayleigh	52	253										
Kelly	53	261	15	72	47	215						
Harriet	54	268										
Ashleigh	55	272										
Catherine	56	276	37	173	22	113	19	90	26	117	42	118
Leah	57	288	99	602								
Nicola	58	300	12	70	3	39	27	120	97	563		
Francesca	59	303										
Naomi	60	306	67	374								

	1994		1984		1974		1964		1954		1944	
	Rank	1 in	Rank	1 in	Rank	1 in	Rank	1 in	Rank	1 in	Rank	1 in
Kate	61	309	44	192	75	408						
Abbie	62	330										
Claire	63	336	6	55	2	35	55	220				
Leanne	64	339	26	130	91	500						
Rachael	65	342	48	212	59	288						
Rosie	66	360										
Aimee	67	362	85	481								
Ellie	68	370										
Sian	69	371	74	397								
Kimberley	70	375	43	192								
Lydia	71	380										
Hollie	72	384										
Stacey	73	387	32	161								
Bethan	74	393										
Amelia	75	395										
Beth	76	403										
Kathryn	77	420	50	246	49	224	60	242	60	258		
Heather	78	429	58	294	72	398	59	238	56	236	57	275
Lisa	79	429	14	70	5	45	54	218				
Helen	80	438	21	99	8	60	8	66	22	104	45	192
Ella	81	443										
Robyn	82	460										
Chantelle	83	479										
Ellen	84	484										
Daisy	85	492										
Demi	86	510										
Courtney	87	530										
Gabrielle	88	535										
Yasmin	89	537										
Lily	90	554										
Rhiannon	91	558										
Maria	92	567	78	430	44	204	30	126	42	170	57	275
Kerry	93	577	35	168	31	139						
Imogen	94	581										
Rebekah	95	598										

	1994		1984		1974		1964		1954		1944	
	Rank	1 in	Rank	1 in	Rank	1 in	Rank	1 in	Rank	1 in	Rank	1 in
Jordan	96	603										
Joanna	97	611	34	165	39	178	90	443				
Caitlin	98	650										
Jemma	99	663	56	285								
Toni	100	683	100	607								
Michelle			18	79	7	55	31	127				
Joanne			23	100	6	45	22	107				
Donna			28	155	25	119	42	158				
Clare			30	159	15	86	72	304				
Jenna			45	193								
Caroline			46	204	19	99	15	84	62	265	95	579
Amanda			49	216	11	67	16	87	85	470		
Karen			51	267	10	66	3	38	37	146		
Alison			54	280	21	105	14	77	53	220		
Sara			55	284	52	242	82	367				
Carly			57	291								
Ruth			60	313	56	273	62	249	65	281	65	316
Fiona			61	323	46	210	44	161	91	518		
Angela			63	330	28	127	12	74	20	97	37	150
Suzanne			64	346	37	170	51	196	84	457		
Katy			65	347								
Marie			66	348	45	209	66	280	57	236	60	280
Cheryl			68	374	66	359	84	379	92	533		
Melanie			69	375	32	144	65	266				
Julie			71	386	14	81	2	32	27	119	92	574
Sally			70	386	33	146	29	126	50	198	85	530
Charlene			72	387								
Tracey			75	410	26	127	6	57				
Deborah			77	416	24	115	5	48	59	255		
Lindsey			79	431	99	571						
Lindsay			81	440								
Susan			82	445	20	105	1	32	1	17	7	47
Jane			86	487	29	129	7	64	12	71	53	236
Kim			87	506	87	470	56	223				
Carla			88	509								

	1994		1984		1974		1964		1954		1944	
	Rank	in	Rank	in	Rank	in	Rank	in	Rank	in	Rank	in
Christine			89	520	63	319	26	117	3	34	3	36
Dawn			90	525	35	158	25	112	86	503		
Tanya			91	535	88	475						
Jenny			92	536								
Andrea			93	538	36	162	52	197	99	602		
Lyndsey			94	542								
Jacqueline			95	565	50	224	4	47	13	77	25	94
Lynsey			96	566								
Mary			98	585	77	409	37	145	9	69	4	42
Marian									51	204	81	514
Sharon					17	94	10	68	63	267		
Tracy					27	127	11	72				
Paula					42	187	33	135				
Wendy					51	241	23	110	32	128	29	108
Lorraine					57	283	35	144	48	186		
Tina					58	284	49	189				
Anne					60	301	34	143	10	70	20	79
Julia					64	338	57	228	55	236	70	389
Gillian					65	356	28	124	16	88	23	87
Vanessa					68	364						
Ann					69	367	40	149	11	71	6	46
Jayne					70	370	50	190				
Diane					71	388	9	68	33	129	35	129
Sandra					73	398	17	88	15	83	13	58
Teresa					74	400	58	236	54	231	83	523
Linda					76	408	18	90	2	33	24	93
Elaine					78	421	43	159	18	93	50	226
Nichola					83	450						
Carol					84	452	21	96	7	60	12	54
Heidi					86	466						
Patricia					89	485	36	145	6	48	2	26
Beverley					90	494	41	157	75	348		
Denise					92	517	38	148	29	123	79	486
Tara					93	527						
Clair					94	536						

	1994		1984		1974		1964		1954		1944	
	Rank	1 in	Rank	1 in	Rank	1 in	Rank	1 in	Rank	1 in	Rank	1 in
Sonia					95	543						
Debbie					96	545	92	451				
Lesley					97	555	46	169	19	95	55	250
Anita					98	571	87	408	95	546	78	483
Debra					100	591	32	131				
Janet							24	111	5	48	8	50
Margaret							39	149	4	46	1	22
Mandy							48	184				
Pauline							53	217	17	89	14	59
Lynn							61	244	36	142		
Yvonne							63	259	38	153	43	189
Judith							64	261	31	126	30	110
Pamela							67	286	21	97	17	65
Carole							68	289	44	181	26	95
Barbara							69	292	14	77	10	53
Gail							70	300	76	364		
Lynne							71	300	39	161		
Janice							73	305	35	134	49	218
Jill							75	315	71	320	63	292
Kathleen							77	343	28	122	19	76
Shirley							78	344	40	164	39	159
Annette							79	347	74	344		
Carolyn							80	351	80	408	76	479
Valerie							83	368	24	113	11	53
Jeanette							85	394	83	430	75	467
Kay							86	404	93	533	80	494
Maxine							88	439				
Frances							89	442	69	317	48	216
Theresa							91	445	87	504		
Lynda							93	466	49	195	73	423
Maureen							94	473	30	125	9	51
Rosemary							95	475	43	174	36	145
Michele							96	493				
Sheila							99	505	34	130	21	79
Jean									25	114	5	46

	1994		1984		1974		1964		1954		1944	
	Rank	I in	Rank	I in	Rank	I in	Rank	I in	Rank	I in	Rank	I in
Marion									41	164	40	173
Joan									45	185	16	63
Marilyn									46	185	54	249
June									47	186	32	119
Brenda									52	207	21	79
Eileen									58	244	28	100
Hilary									61	259	62	285
Sylvia									64	280	26	95
Irene									66	295	34	129
Dorothy									67	308	31	111
Josephine									70	320	44	191
Joyce									72	338	33	128
Hazel									73	338	47	211
Rita									77	370	41	175
Geraldine									78	391	98	604
Diana									79	395	51	232
Christina									81	421	74	447
Penelope									82	427	72	401
Joy									89	509	90	556
Doreen									90	511	38	152
Glynis									94	542		
Veronica									98	568	52	235
Audrey									100	607	67	341
Beryl											46	193
Norma											56	257
Gloria											59	279
Marjorie											61	282
Cynthia											64	306
Mavis											66	332
Marlene											68	378
Betty											69	384
Evelyn											71	394
Iris											77	482
Vera											82	517
Bridget											87	535

	1994		1984		1974		1964		1954		1944	
	Rank	1 in	Rank	1 in	Rank	1 in	Rank	1 in	Rank	1 in	Rank	1 in
Lilian											88	554
Monica											89	556
Glenys											91	565
Vivienne											93	574
Daphne											94	576
Phyllis											96	583
Gwendoline											97	601
Doris											99	610
Muriel											100	629

2.5. Ranking and frequency: boys' names 1–100

Commentary and overview

Traditionally parents have tended to be more conservative when naming boys, a tendency which is confirmed by studying these tables. However there has been much more variety in recent years, and it may in future be easy to date the ages of boys as much as girls by their name. There seems to be a well-used central stock of boys' names; indeed in 1994 the Top 100 boys' names were given to 3 in every 4 baby boys.

The following names appear in all years: Thomas, James, Daniel, Michael, Alexander, Christopher, Joseph, William, Andrew, George, David, Robert, Jonathan, John, Mohammed, Nicholas, Charles, Edward, Stephen, Richard, Peter, Anthony, Paul, Patrick, Timothy, Philip, Martin and Stuart. As explained in Appendix A, the names of people migrating to England and Wales are included, which when added to those who are born in this country show that the name Mohammed, and some of its variations, has become increasingly popular.

Making a comeback in 1994 were Harry, Henry, Marcus and Christian.

New entries were Jake, Callum, Jacob, Kyle, Joe, Reece, Rhys, Charlie, Cameron, Louis, Conor, Elliot, Max, Mitchell, Billy, Joel, Josh, Dylan, Elliott, Brandon, Toby, Tom, Declan, Jay, and Owen.

On their way up are Thomas, James, Jack, Daniel, Matthew, Ryan, Joshua, Luke, Samuel, Jordan, Adam, Alexander, Benjamin, Joseph, Liam, William, George, Lewis, Oliver, Jamie, Nathan, Aaron, Ashley, Bradley, Kieran, Scott, Sam, Ben, Mohammed, Charles, Sean, Edward, Alex, Dominic and Dale.

On their way down are Michael, Christopher, Andrew, David, Robert, Jonathan, John, Nicholas, Mark, Stephen, Richard, Peter, Lee, Anthony, Paul, Craig, Jason, Ross, Dean, Patrick, Shaun, Simon, Timothy, Philip, Carl, Martin, Stuart, Gareth, Danny, Karl, Mohammad, Mathew, Darren.

In decline after 1944 are Alfred, Barrie, Cyril, Edwin, Ernest, Harold, Ivan, Melvyn, Ralph, Reginald, Rodney, Royston, Sidney and Walter.

16 names are pushed out after 1954: Albert, Arthur, Bernard, Bryan, Clifford, Denis, Frank, Frederick, Hugh, Lawrence, Leonard, Maurice, Mohamed, Norman, Stanley and Victor.

Out of favour after the swinging sixties' are Allan, Bruce, Clive, Dennis, Donald, Douglas, Eric, Francis, Geoffrey, Gerald, Gerard, Gordon, Graeme, Guy, Howard, Jeffrey, Leslie and Ronald.

The seventies child may have been called Brett, Damian, Derek, Duncan, Garry, Glen, Glenn, Jeremy, Julian, Kenneth, Malcolm, Nigel, Raymond, Roger, Terence and Trevor.

Future twenty-first century boys are Abdul, Adrian, Alan, Antony, Barry, Brian, Colin, Damien, Gary, Gavin, Graham, Gregory, Iain, Ian, Justin, Keith, Kevin, Leigh, Leon, Marc, Martyn, Neil, Phillip, Ricky, Robin, Russell, Stewart, Terry, Tony and Wayne.

Table 2
Top 100 boys' names,
1944–1994, England and Wales

Example: Jack is 3rd in 1994, given to 1 in 33 babies in that year. But if you look at the 1984 columns you will see that it was 74th in that year, given to 1 in 476 babies. If you want to know when it entered the Top 100, scan across the other columns. You will see that the 1954, 1964 and 1974 columns are blank, but the 1944 columns are filled. So you know Jack appeared for the first time in the Top 100 in 1944, disappeared for 3 decades and reappeared in 1984.

	1994		1984		1974		1964		1954		1944	
	Rank	1 in	Rank	1 in	Rank	1 in	Rank	1 in	Rank	1 in	Rank	1 in
Thomas	1	29	11	48	40	182	34	185	24	112	19	81
James	2	31	2	28	7	41	19	75	14	63	10	48
Jack	3	33	74	476							81	526
Daniel	4	33	4	30	16	56	53	313	73	526	82	556
Matthew	5	40	6	35	10	46	52	313				
Ryan	6	42	28	128	79	588						
Joshua	7	42	78	556								
Luke	8	48	29	130	95	714						
Samuel	9	51	43	161	82	588					97	833
Jordan	10	57	93	769								
Adam	11	59	12	53	35	167	68	435				
Michael	12	60	5	34	9	45	6	30	4	24	3	19
Alexander	13	62	25	111	43	217	77	556	71	526	66	435
Christopher	14	64	1	25	6	40	11	46	9	51	16	73
Benjamin	15	67	16	68	34	154						
Joseph	16	68	40	154	59	370	48	294	47	222	36	164
Liam	17	76	56	238								
Jake	18	79										
William	19	82	34	137	41	208	29	132	15	63	9	44
Andrew	20	85	7	35	4	29	3	21	12	57	45	196
George	21	89	71	435	83	625	54	333	35	159	21	87
Lewis	22	91	66	400								
Oliver	23	92	48	192	84	625						
David	24	95	3	29	3	29	1	18	1	16	2	14
Robert	25	99	13	55	14	54	9	45	6	32	5	34

	1994		1984		1974		1964		1954		1944	
	Rank	1 in	Rank	1 in	Rank	1 in	Rank	1 in	Rank	1 in	Rank	1 in
Jamie	26	103	30	133	45	222						
Nathan	27	106	57	244	58	370						
Connor	28	118										
Jonathan	29	122	18	73	20	69	27	127	52	286		
Harry	30	123							100	1000	65	417
Callum	31	125										
Aaron	32	133	53	222								
Ashley	33	135	49	192								
Bradley	34	149	92	769								
Jacob	35	152										
Kieran	36	152	90	714								
Scott	37	161	38	149	31	118						
Sam	38	161	72	455								
John	39	164	14	62	13	51	5	27	2	18	1	12
Ben	40	169	45	175								
Mohammed	41	175	54	227	61	385	73	526	56	323	87	625
Nicholas	42	182	22	88	19	69	28	130	36	161	76	476
Kyle	43	192										
Charles	44	192	69	417	70	476	56	357	38	172	38	172
Mark	45	196	10	46	2	25	4	24	32	154		
Sean	46	196	46	185	56	323	36	233				
Edward	47	208	51	213	52	278	49	303	45	196	29	118
Stephen	48	208	20	79	11	48	7	32	3	23	40	179
Richard	49	213	8	46	5	40	10	46	10	54	11	57
Alex	50	217	79	556								
Peter	51	217	23	95	23	85	12	47	5	28	4	24
Dominic	52	238	80	556	69	455	100	909				
Joe	53	244										
Reece	54	244										
Lee	55	244	15	63	12	51	50	303				
Rhys	56	250										
Steven	57	250	17	72	17	58	17	70	23	106		
Anthony	58	256	24	108	25	88	14	60	11	54	6	40
Charlie	59	256										
Paul	60	270	9	46	1	24	2	18	7	32	28	100

	1994		1984		1974		1964		1954		1944	
	Rank	1 in	Rank	1 in	Rank	1 in	Rank	1 in	Rank	1 in	Rank	1 in
Craig	61	286	19	75	28	100	60	370				
Jason	62	286	41	159	18	67	93	833				
Dale	63	286	76	526								
Ross	64	294	60	313								
Cameron	65	303										
Louis	66	303										
Dean	67	323	39	152	37	172	44	278				
Conor	68	333										
Shane	69	357	70	417	65	417						
Elliot	70	357										
Patrick	71	357	65	370	67	435	35	189	39	179	31	143
Max	72	357										
Shaun	73	357	52	222	57	333	40	256				
Henry	74	357							83	667	63	417
Simon	75	370	21	79	8	43	13	58	53	294		
Timothy	76	385	47	185	33	149	24	111	40	179	77	476
Mitchell	77	417										
Billy	78	435										
Philip	79	455	32	135	29	106	20	84	16	63	32	145
Joel	80	455										
Josh	81	476										
Marcus	82	476			71	476						
Dylan	83	500										
Carl	84	500	44	169	39	179	37	233				
Elliott	85	526										
Brandon	86	526										
Martin	87	588	36	141	26	94	18	73	21	89	41	182
Toby	88	588										
Stuart	89	588	31	133	24	88	32	139	49	244	55	270
Gareth	90	588	35	141	46	250	79	588	85	714		
Danny	91	588	86	625								
Christian	92	588			49	270						
Tom	93	625										
Declan	94	625										
Karl	95	625	61	323	50	270	64	400				

	1994		1984		1974		1964		1954		1944	
	Rank	1 in	Rank	1 in	Rank	1 in	Rank	1 in	Rank	1 in	Rank	1 in
Mohammad	96	667	83	588					84	667		
Mathew	97	667	73	455	87	667						
Jay	98	667										
Owen	99	667										
Darren	100	714	33	135	15	55	66	417				
Gary			26	127	30	108	16	63	34	159	95	833
Ian			27	128	21	70	8	41	13	60	23	88
Kevin			37	147	27	96	15	63	20	78	67	435
Neil			42	161	22	82	22	91	46	208	80	500
Wayne			50	204	32	139	39	250				
Gavin			55	238	72	476	97	833				
Alan			58	263	36	169	21	88	8	47	8	44
Graham			59	313	42	213	26	115	19	75	22	87
Marc			62	323	54	286						
Adrian			63	345	38	172	30	133	54	303	74	476
Phillip			64	357	63	400	59	357	57	333	93	769
Colin			67	400	44	222	25	114	22	91	15	69
Russell			68	417	60	370	55	333				
Ricky			75	500								
Tony			77	526	73	476	67	417	79	625	96	833
Barry			81	556	48	270	42	270	33	156	20	85
Leon			82	556	91	667						
Terry			84	588	93	714	86	714	92	833	88	625
Gregory			85	588	81	588	78	588	94	833		
Brian			87	625	51	278	31	139	17	72	7	42
Keith			88	667	53	278	33	141	18	74	14	69
Antony			89	667	74	500	46	286	99	909		
Justin			91	714	47	263						
Martyn			94	769	80	588	87	714	75	588		
Leigh			95	833	98	714						
Abdul			96	833	86	667			74	556		
Damien			97	833								
Stewart			98	833	88	667	83	667	91	833		
Robin			99	833	75	526	69	455	59	345	57	278
Iain			100	909	78	588	94	833				

	1994		1984		1974		1964		1954		1944	
	Rank	I in	Rank	I in	Rank	I in	Rank	I in	Rank	I in	Rank	I in
Nigel					55	323	23	110	27	125	69	435
Jeremy					62	385	47	294	70	500		
Damian					64	417						
Duncan					66	435	75	556				
Julian					68	455	62	370	96	909		
Trevor					76	556	38	244	30	139	33	145
Glen					77	556						
Raymond					85	625	45	286	26	122	17	74
Malcolm					89	667	65	400	31	139	24	92
Garry					90	667	70	476	82	667		
Brett					92	667						
Kenneth					94	714	41	263	25	120	12	63
Roger					96	714	61	370	41	182	13	66
Glenn					97	714	95	833	98	909		
Terence					99	714	51	303	29	137	18	81
Derek					100	769	43	278	37	164	27	99
Jeffrey							57	357	48	233	51	250
Clive							58	357	44	196	50	227
Geoffrey							63	370	28	130	25	93
Roy							71	476	50	250	30	125
Vincent							72	500	87	769	94	769
Gordon							74	526	51	278	44	192
Leslie							76	556	42	182	35	164
Ronald							80	625	43	192	26	96
Douglas							81	625	69	476	52	256
Francis							82	625	61	357	54	263
Graeme							84	667				
Guy							85	667				
Eric							88	714	62	357	39	175
Allan							89	714	58	333	58	286
Gerard							90	769	78	588		
Gerald							91	833	60	357	49	222
Howard							92	833	68	455	64	417
Dennis							96	833	55	313	34	164
Bruce							98	909			92	714

	1994	1984	1974	1964	1954	1944
	Rank 1 in	Rank 1 in	Rank 1 in	Rank 1 in	Rank 1 in	Rank 1 in
Donald				99 909	64 417	53 263
Bernard					63 400	37 172
Frank					65 435	46 208
Norman					66 435	43 189
Frederick					67 435	42 182
Arthur					72 526	47 217
Leonard					76 588	59 323
Lawrence					77 588	83 556
Bryan					80 625	79 500
Clifford					81 625	68 435
Stanley					86 769	60 333
Victor					88 769	56 270
Hugh					89 769	84 588
Mohamed					90 769	
Albert					93 833	61 345
Maurice					95 833	62 400
Denis					97 909	85 558
Rodney						48 217
Barrie						70 435
Reginald						71 435
Ernest						72 455
Alfred						73 455
Harold						75 476
Melvyn						78 476
Walter						86 625
Edwin						89 667
Ralph						90 714
Ivan						91 714
Cyril						98 909
Sidney						99 909
Royston						100 909

2.6. Ranking and number: girls' names A–Z

Commentary and overview

The Top 100 girls' names are listed in the following pages in their alphabetical order for each year in Table 3. The number of occurrences is given for each name to enable absolute comparisons to be made across years. For ranking and frequencies, you can refer to Table 1, Top 100 girls' names.

Did you know that a girl born in 1994 is most likely to have the initial A as 10 of the Top 100 names begin with A? Or that in a group of women born in 1954 you would be twice as likely to find yourself next to someone named Susan than someone named Linda or Christine, and you would have a 1 in 17 chance of being next to Susan in the first place? In contrast, in 1994, the gap between the 1st and 2nd names Rebecca and Lauren was only 233 baby girls.

Figure A (opposite) shows the number of occurrences of the 1st and 100th names in the selected years. Susan is the 'biggest' top name with 22,897 occurrences; 1994's Rebecca is the smallest with only 8,256 occurrences. In 1994 the top name Rebecca was given to 8,256 girls while the 100th name was only given to 483 girls. This was the smallest gap between the 1st and 100th name; again Susan paved the way in 1,954 by being given to 22,897 girls while Audrey was only given to 638 girls.

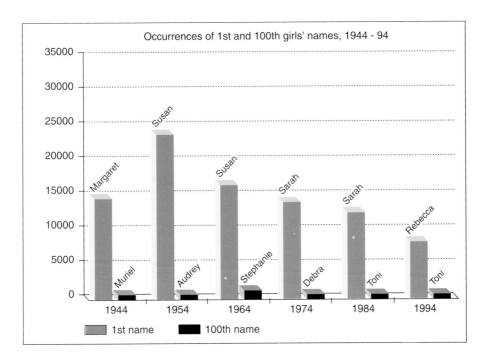

Table 3
Alphabetical Top 100 girls' names,
1944–1994, England and Wales

	1994			1984			1974	
Name	Rank	**Number**	**Name**	Rank	**Number**	**Name**	Rank	**Number**
Abbie	62	999	Abigail	80	756	Alexandra	82	804
Abigail	23	2524	Aimee	85	689	Alison	21	3330
Aimee	67	911	Alexandra	52	1228	Amanda	11	5204
Alexandra	40	1796	Alice	83	709	Andrea	36	2160
Alice	18	3350	Alison	54	1185	Angela	28	2749
Amber	50	1328	Amanda	49	1538	Anita	98	614
Amelia	75	835	Amy	10	5171	Ann	69	955
Amy	7	6252	Andrea	93	617	Anna	40	1885
Anna	48	1364	Angela	63	1006	Anne	60	1163
Ashleigh	55	1212	Anna	39	1870	Beverley	90	709
Beth	76	819	Carla	88	652	Carol	84	775
Bethan	74	839	Carly	57	1141	Caroline	19	3530
Bethany	15	3751	Caroline	46	1627	Catherine	22	3107
Caitlin	98	507	Catherine	37	1920	Charlotte	41	1883
Catherine	56	1196	Charlene	72	857	Cheryl	66	977
Chantelle	83	689	Charlotte	22	3335	Christine	63	1097
Charlotte	4	7337	Cheryl	68	886	Clair	94	653
Chelsea	38	1818	Chloe	97	581	Claire	2	9943
Chloe	11	4575	Christine	89	638	Clare	15	4054
Claire	63	981	Claire	6	6003	Dawn	35	2216
Courtney	87	622	Clare	30	2080	Debbie	96	643
Daisy	85	670	Danielle	27	2323	Deborah	24	3051
Danielle	21	2924	Dawn	90	632	Debra	100	593
Demi	86	647	Deborah	77	797	Denise	92	677
Eleanor	32	2149	Donna	28	2145	Diane	71	903
Elizabeth	26	2307	Eleanor	76	807	Donna	25	2940
Ella	81	745	Elizabeth	25	2750	Elaine	78	833
Ellen	84	681	Emily	36	1945	Elizabeth	23	3063
Ellie	68	891	Emma	4	8334	Emily	80	814
Emily	8	5816	Fiona	61	1026	Emma	4	8109

	1964			1954			1944	
Name	Rank	**Number**	**Name**	Rank	**Number**	**Name**	Rank	**Number**
Alison	14	6499	Alison	53	1761	Angela	37	2483
Amanda	16	5786	Amanda	85	824	Anita	78	773
Andrea	52	2549	Andrea	99	643	Ann	6	8034
Angela	12	6779	Angela	20	3988	Anne	20	4738
Anita	87	1233	Anita	95	709	Audrey	67	1094
Ann	40	3371	Ann	11	5490	Barbara	10	7007
Anna	81	1370	Anna	88	767	Beryl	46	1939
Anne	34	3517	Anne	10	5516	Betty	69	972
Annette	79	1448	Annette	74	1127	Brenda	22	4701
Barbara	69	1725	Audrey	100	638	Bridget	87	698
Beverley	41	3203	Barbara	14	5008	Carol	12	6876
Carol	21	5222	Beverley	75	1112	Carole	27	3911
Carole	68	1740	Brenda	52	1869	Caroline	95	645
Caroline	15	5955	Carol	7	6440	Carolyn	76	779
Carolyn	80	1433	Carole	44	2140	Catherine	42	1988
Catherine	19	5557	Caroline	62	1459	Christina	74	836
Cheryl	84	1328	Carolyn	80	949	Christine	3	10265
Christine	26	4297	Catherine	26	3304	Cynthia	64	1219
Claire	55	2281	Cheryl	92	727	Daphne	94	648
Clare	72	1656	Christina	81	920	Denise	79	769
Dawn	25	4470	Christine	3	11489	Diana	51	1610
Debbie	92	1114	Dawn	86	769	Diane	35	2893
Deborah	5	10409	Deborah	59	1521	Doreen	38	2459
Debra	32	3825	Denise	29	3138	Doris	99	612
Denise	38	3408	Diana	79	980	Dorothy	31	3367
Diane	9	7431	Diane	33	3007	Eileen	28	3735
Donna	42	3183	Doreen	90	757	Elaine	50	1652
Elaine	43	3160	Dorothy	67	1255	Elizabeth	15	6239
Elizabeth	20	5493	Eileen	58	1584	Evelyn	71	947
Fiona	44	3122	Elaine	18	4153	Frances	48	1728

	1994			1984			1974	
Name	Rank	**Number**	**Name**	Rank	**Number**	**Name**	Rank	**Number**
Emma	10	5375	Gemma	3	8399	Fiona	46	1671
Francesca	59	1090	Georgina	84	706	Georgina	79	817
Gabrielle	88	616	Hannah	20	3633	Gillian	65	984
Gemma	36	1902	Hayley	19	3711	Hannah	67	976
Georgia	29	2193	Heather	58	1129	Hayley	53	1437
Georgina	35	1942	Helen	21	3365	Heather	72	881
Grace	47	1403	Holly	59	1089	Heidi	86	752
Hannah	5	7286	Jacqueline	95	587	Helen	8	5804
Harriet	54	1229	Jade	73	856	Jacqueline	50	1561
Hayley	43	1527	Jane	86	681	Jane	29	2710
Heather	78	769	Jemma	56	1162	Jayne	70	947
Helen	80	753	Jenna	45	1718	Jennifer	34	2385
Hollie	72	859	Jennifer	11	4921	Joanna	39	1971
Holly	22	2560	Jenny	92	619	Joanne	6	7711
Imogen	94	568	Jessica	40	1850	Julia	64	1035
Jade	16	3661	Joanna	34	2006	Julie	14	4341
Jasmine	51	1311	Joanne	23	3320	Karen	10	5268
Jemma	99	497	Jodie	53	1200	Kate	75	858
Jennifer	42	1544	Julie	71	859	Katherine	43	1772
Jessica	3	7583	Karen	51	1240	Kathryn	49	1562
Joanna	97	540	Kate	44	1727	Katie	81	807
Jodie	46	1463	Katherine	29	2131	Kelly	47	1632
Jordan	96	547	Kathryn	50	1350	Kerry	31	2520
Kate	61	1068	Katie	13	4753	Kim	87	746
Katherine	45	1491	Katy	65	956	Kirsty	62	1136
Kathryn	77	785	Kelly	15	4635	Laura	54	1426
Katie	14	3906	Kerry	35	1972	Leanne	91	700
Kayleigh	52	1301	Kim	87	655	Lesley	97	631
Kelly	53	1262	Kimberley	43	1732	Linda	76	858
Kerry	93	571	Kirsty	42	1824	Lindsey	99	614
Kimberley	70	880	Laura	2	9682	Lisa	5	7735
Kirsty	39	1810	Lauren	33	2020	Lorraine	57	1240
Laura	9	5442	Leah	99	551	Louise	13	4861
Lauren	2	8023	Leanne	26	2546	Lucy	38	2036
Leah	57	1145	Lindsay	81	753	Maria	44	1717

	1964			1954			1944	
Name	Rank	**Number**	**Name**	Rank	**Number**	**Name**	Rank	**Number**
Frances	89	1138	Elizabeth	8	6342	Georgina	84	708
Gail	70	1678	Fiona	91	748	Geraldine	98	618
Gillian	28	4069	Frances	69	1221	Gillian	23	4274
Heather	59	2117	Gail	76	1065	Glenys	91	661
Helen	8	7662	Geraldine	78	991	Gloria	59	1336
Jacqueline	4	10770	Gillian	16	4420	Gwendoline	97	621
Jane	7	7818	Glynis	94	714	Hazel	47	1772
Janet	24	4540	Hazel	73	1145	Heather	58	1356
Janice	73	1651	Heather	56	1641	Helen	45	1949
Jayne	50	2641	Helen	22	3706	Hilary	62	1310
Jeanette	85	1276	Hilary	61	1497	Irene	34	2903
Jennifer	45	3103	Irene	66	1312	Iris	77	774
Jill	75	1594	Jacqueline	13	5014	Jacqueline	25	3958
Joanna	90	1134	Jane	12	5447	Jane	53	1580
Joanne	22	4716	Janet	5	8044	Janet	8	7417
Judith	64	1923	Janice	35	2899	Janice	49	1709
Julia	57	2203	Jean	25	3397	Jean	5	8047
Julie	2	15593	Jeanette	83	901	Jeanette	75	800
Karen	3	13324	Jennifer	23	3566	Jennifer	18	5643
Katherine	76	1504	Jill	71	1209	Jill	63	1280
Kathleen	77	1465	Joan	45	2092	Joan	16	5907
Kathryn	60	2079	Josephine	70	1211	Josephine	44	1956
Kay	86	1246	Joy	89	760	Joy	90	671
Kim	56	2253	Joyce	72	1147	Joyce	33	2925
Laura	97	1004	Judith	31	3074	Judith	30	3379
Lesley	46	2976	Julia	55	1642	Julia	70	959
Linda	18	5567	Julie	27	3262	Julie	92	650
Lisa	54	2310	June	47	2086	June	32	3138
Lorraine	35	3483	Karen	37	2644	Kathleen	19	4889
Louise	47	2811	Kathleen	28	3178	Kay	80	756
Lynda	93	1079	Kathryn	60	1500	Lesley	55	1491
Lynn	61	2057	Kay	93	727	Lilian	88	674
Lynne	71	1677	Lesley	19	4066	Linda	24	4025
Mandy	48	2736	Linda	2	11755	Lynda	73	882
Margaret	39	3374	Lorraine	48	2076	Margaret	1	17226

	1994			1984			1974	
Name	Rank	Number	Name	Rank	Number	Name	Rank	Number
Leanne	64	973	Lindsey	79	770	Marie	45	1677
Lily	90	595	Lisa	14	4744	Mary	77	856
Lisa	79	768	Louise	17	4324	Melanie	32	2431
Louise	44	1495	Lucy	24	3175	Michelle	7	6398
Lucy	13	4090	Lyndsey	94	612	Natalie	48	1628
Lydia	71	867	Lynsey	96	586	Natasha	55	1292
Maria	92	582	Maria	78	772	Nichola	83	779
Megan	17	3653	Marie	66	952	Nicola	3	8993
Melissa	41	1640	Mary	98	567	Patricia	89	723
Naomi	60	1077	Melissa	62	1015	Rachael	59	1216
Natalie	31	2185	Michelle	18	4198	Rachel	12	5042
Natasha	28	2220	Naomi	67	888	Rebecca	16	3855
Nicola	58	1100	Natalie	16	4585	Ruth	56	1282
Nicole	37	1853	Natasha	47	1563	Sally	33	2394
Olivia	24	2427	Nicola	12	4755	Samantha	9	5299
Paige	34	1955	Rachael	48	1563	Sandra	73	881
Rachael	65	964	Rachel	9	5229	Sara	52	1449
Rachel	19	3094	Rebecca	5	7405	Sarah	1	13285
Rebecca	1	8256	Ruth	60	1058	Sharon	17	3742
Rebekah	95	551	Sally	70	859	Sonia	95	645
Rhiannon	91	591	Samantha	8	5546	Sophie	85	761
Robyn	82	717	Sara	55	1167	Stephanie	61	1139
Rosie	66	917	Sarah	1	11391	Susan	20	3348
Samantha	20	2993	Sian	74	835	Suzanne	37	2065
Sarah	12	4320	Sophie	38	1872	Tanya	88	737
Shannon	33	1979	Stacey	32	2059	Tara	93	665
Sian	69	889	Stephanie	31	2069	Teresa	74	875
Sophie	6	6970	Susan	82	746	Tina	58	1232
Stacey	73	853	Suzanne	64	960	Tracey	26	2769
Stephanie	25	2392	Tanya	91	620	Tracy	27	2759
Toni	100	483	Toni	100	546	Vanessa	68	962
Victoria	27	2223	Tracey	75	808	Victoria	18	3696
Yasmin	89	614	Victoria	7	5703	Wendy	51	1456
Zoe	30	2192	Zoe	41	1830	Zoe	30	2546

Top 100 boys' names,
Wales

	1984			1974	
Name	Rank	**Number**	**Name**	Rank	**Number**
Aaron	53	1564	Abdul	86	548
Abdul	96	418	Adam	35	2136
Adam	12	6561	Adrian	38	2076
Adrian	63	1008	Alan	36	2114
Alan	58	1317	Alexander	43	1626
Alex	79	633	Andrew	4	12354
Alexander	25	3113	Anthony	25	4030
Andrew	7	9850	Antony	74	708
Anthony	24	3220	Barry	48	1318
Antony	89	509	Benjamin	34	2327
Ashley	49	1803	Brett	92	521
Barry	81	626	Brian	51	1301
Ben	45	1981	Carl	39	1985
enjamin	16	5061	Charles	70	752
Bradley	92	466	Christian	49	1318
Brian	87	547	Christopher	6	9053
Carl	44	2040	Colin	44	1602
Charles	69	824	Craig	28	3579
topher	1	13966	Damien	64	869
Colin	67	853	Daniel	16	6441
Craig	19	4622	Darren	15	6489
Dale	76	669	David	3	12423
mien	97	412	Dean	37	2082
aniel	4	11578	Derek	100	476
anny	86	550	Dominic	69	790
rren	33	2568	Duncan	66	815
avid	3	11854	Edward	52	1301
ean	39	2286	Gareth	46	1435
inic	80	632	Garry	90	533
ard	51	1639	Gary	30	3308

	1964			1954			1944	
Name	Rank	**Number**	**Name**	Rank	**Number**	**Name**	Rank	**Number**
Maria	30	3995	Lynda	49	1985	Maria	57	1358
Marie	66	1795	Lynn	36	2733	Marian	81	726
Mary	37	3458	Lynne	39	2406	Marie	60	1335
Maureen	94	1064	Margaret	4	8495	Marilyn	54	1499
Maxine	88	1146	Maria	42	2272	Marion	40	2153
Melanie	65	1893	Marian	51	1902	Marjorie	61	1324
Michele	96	1020	Marie	57	1640	Marlene	68	989
Michelle	31	3965	Marilyn	46	2092	Mary	4	8868
Nicola	27	4202	Marion	41	2360	Maureen	9	7368
Patricia	36	3467	Maureen	30	3090	Monica	89	672
Paula	33	3735	Nicola	97	688	Muriel	100	594
Pauline	53	2322	Pamela	21	3972	Norma	56	1454
Rachel	74	1642	Patricia	6	8037	Pamela	17	5742
Rebecca	98	997	Pauline	17	4374	Patricia	2	14222
Rosemary	95	1058	Penelope	82	907	Pauline	14	6355
Ruth	62	2020	Rita	77	1046	Penelope	72	931
Sally	29	4003	Rosemary	43	2225	Phyllis	96	640
Sandra	17	5727	Ruth	65	1376	Rita	41	2131
Sara	82	1370	Sally	50	1957	Rosemary	36	2574
Sarah	13	6761	Sandra	15	4681	Ruth	65	1181
Sharon	10	7351	Sarah	68	1250	Sally	85	704
Sheila	99	996	Sharon	63	1450	Sandra	13	6414
Shirley	78	1461	Sheila	34	2985	Sarah	86	699
Stephanie	100	972	Shirley	40	2367	Sheila	21	4722
Susan	1	15868	Stephanie	96	702	Shirley	39	2355
Suzanne	51	2561	Susan	1	22897	Susan	7	7940
Teresa	58	2131	Suzanne	84	847	Sylvia	26	3912
Theresa	91	1129	Sylvia	64	1385	Teresa	83	714
Tina	49	2664	Teresa	54	1677	Valerie	11	7000
Tracey	6	8876	Theresa	87	768	Vera	82	722
Tracy	11	6997	Valerie	24	3428	Veronica	52	1587
Valerie	83	1368	Veronica	98	682	Vivienne	93	650
Wendy	23	4580	Wendy	32	3027	Wendy	29	3448
Yvonne	63	1939	Yvonne	38	2526	Yvonne	43	1972

2.7. Ranking and number: boys' names A–Z

Commentary and overview

The Top 100 Boys' names are listed in the following pages in their alphabetical order each of the years in Table 4. The number of occurrences is given for each name to enable absolute comparisons to be made across years. For ranking and frequencies, you can refer to Table 2, Top 100 boys' names.

Did you know that a boy born in 1994 is most likely to have the initial K as 15 of the Top 100 names start with K? Or that in a meeting full of men born in 1944 you would have a 1 in 12 chance of being next to a man named John? The greatest gap between 1st and 2nd names was 5,434 between John and David in 1944. In contrast in 1994 the gap between Thomas and James was only 795.

Figure B (opposite) shows the number of occurrences of the 1st and 100th names in the selected years. John is the 'biggest' top name with 32,216 occurrences; 1994's Thomas is the 'smallest' with only 11,845 occurrences. In 1994 the top name Thomas was given to 11,845 boys while the 100th name was only given to 499 boys. This was the smallest gap between the 1st and 100th name; again John paved the way in 1944 by being given to 32,216 boys while Royston was only given to 421 boys.

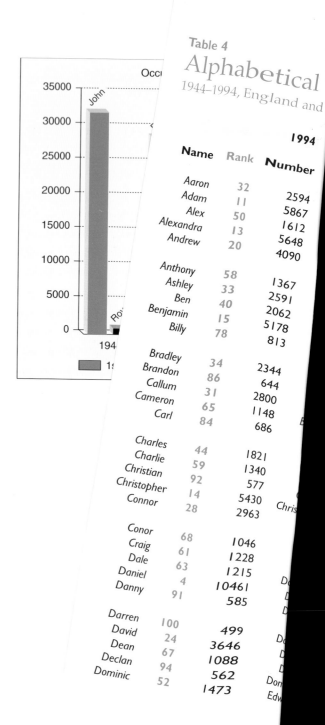

Table 4

Alphabetical
1944–1994, England and

Name	Rank	Number
		1994
Aaron	32	2594
Adam	11	5867
Alex	50	1612
Alexandra	13	5648
Andrew	20	4090
Anthony	58	1367
Ashley	33	2591
Ben	40	2062
Benjamin	15	5178
Billy	78	813
Bradley	34	2344
Brandon	86	644
Callum	31	2800
Cameron	65	1148
Carl	84	686
Charles	44	1821
Charlie	59	1340
Christian	92	577
Christopher	14	5430
Connor	28	2963
Conor	68	1046
Craig	61	1228
Dale	63	1215
Daniel	4	10461
Danny	91	585
Darren	100	499
David	24	3646
Dean	67	1088
Declan	94	562
Dominic	52	1473

	1964			1954			1944	
Name	Rank	**Number**	**Name**	Rank	**Number**	**Name**	Rank	**Number**
Adam	68	1164	Abdul	74	697	Adrian	74	819
Adrian	30	3774	Adrian	54	1318	Alan	8	8693
Alan	21	5752	Alan	8	8355	Albert	61	1120
Alexander	77	914	Albert	93	466	Alexander	66	896
Allan	89	692	Alexander	71	761	Alfred	73	823
Andrew	3	24317	Allan	58	1183	Allan	58	1336
Anthony	14	8379	Andrew	12	6852	Andrew	45	1940
Antony	46	1760	Anthony	11	7305	Anthony	6	9495
Barry	42	1846	Antony	99	422	Arthur	47	1756
Brian	31	3660	Arthur	72	758	Barrie	70	868
Bruce	98	565	Barry	33	2543	Barry	20	4456
Carl	37	2178	Bernard	63	983	Bernard	37	2217
Charles	56	1425	Brian	17	5442	Brian	7	9104
Christopher	11	10905	Bryan	80	632	Bruce	92	516
Clive	58	1396	Charles	38	2289	Bryan	79	750
Colin	25	4431	Christopher	9	7768	Charles	38	2216
Craig	60	1375	Clifford	81	622	Christopher	16	5239
Daniel	53	1609	Clive	44	2016	Clifford	68	876
Darren	66	1232	Colin	22	4343	Clive	50	1663
David	1	28538	Daniel	73	736	Colin	15	5487
Dean	44	1795	David	1	24266	Cyril	98	433
Dennis	96	590	Denis	97	434	Daniel	82	707
Derek	43	1839	Dennis	55	1281	David	2	26728
Dominic	100	531	Derek	37	2388	Denis	85	648
Donald	99	563	Donald	64	946	Dennis	34	2346
Douglas	81	791	Douglas	69	817	Derek	27	3851
Duncan	75	929	Edward	45	1993	Donald	53	1446
Edward	49	1680	Eric	62	1096	Douglas	52	1480
Eric	88	700	Francis	61	1100	Edward	29	3247
Francis	82	786	Frank	65	923	Edwin	89	572

	1994			1984			1974	
Name	Rank	**Number**	**Name**	Rank	**Number**	**Name**	Rank	**Number**
Dylan	83	688	Gareth	35	2453	Gavin	72	736
Edward	47	1677	Gary	26	2748	George	83	587
Elliot	70	981	Gavin	55	1475	Glen	77	627
Elliott	85	667	George	71	804	Glenn	97	484
Gareth	90	586	Graham	59	1117	Graham	42	1673
George	21	3907	Gregory	85	578	Gregory	81	609
Harry	30	2829	Iain	100	399	Iain	78	624
Henry	74	963	Ian	27	2727	Ian	21	5105
Jack	3	10599	Jack	74	734	James	7	8597
Jacob	35	2300	James	2	12496	Jamie	45	1602
Jake	18	4425	Jamie	30	2620	Jason	18	5332
James	2	11050	Jason	41	2193	Jeremy	62	917
Jamie	26	3359	John	14	5583	John	13	7000
Jason	62	1218	Jonathon	18	4744	Jonathon	20	5164
Jay	98	517	Jordan	93	450	Joseph	59	965
Joe	53	1436	Joseph	40	2269	Julian	68	793
Joel	80	759	Joshua	78	635	Justin	47	1347
John	39	2139	Justin	91	497	Karl	50	1308
Jonathon	29	2860	Karl	61	1081	Keith	53	1279
Jordan	10	6067	Keith	88	512	Kenneth	94	500
Joseph	16	5159	Kevin	37	2375	Kevin	27	3724
Josh	81	725	Kieran	90	503	Lee	12	7032
Joshua	7	8265	Lee	15	5571	Leigh	98	484
Karl	95	557	Leigh	95	422	Leon	91	527
Kieran	36	2288	Leon	82	610	Luke	95	499
Kyle	43	1822	Lewis	66	864	Malcolm	89	536
Lee	55	1412	Liam	56	1452	Marc	54	1253
Lewis	22	3833	Luke	29	2671	Marcus	71	743
Liam	17	4597	Marc	62	1076	Mark	2	14445
Louis	66	1145	Mark	10	7557	Martin	26	3801
Luke	8	7197	Martin	36	2540	Martyn	80	610
Marcus	82	724	Martyn	94	436	Mathew	87	548
Mark	45	1779	Mathew	73	751	Matthew	10	7803
Martin	87	608	Matthew	6	10024	Michael	9	7848
Mathew	97	522	Michael	5	10192	Mohammed	61	928

	1964			**1954**			**1944**	
Name	Rank	**Number**	**Name**	Rank	**Number**	**Name**	Rank	**Number**
Gareth	79	839	Frederick	67	902	Eric	39	2175
Garry	70	1083	Gareth	82	590	Ernest	72	836
Gary	16	8034	Garry	69	1221	Francis	54	1439
Gavin	97	587	Gary	34	2505	Frank	46	1824
Geoffrey	63	1367	Geoffrey	28	3030	Frederick	42	2085
George	54	1509	George	35	2471	Gary	95	472
Gerald	91	617	Gerald	60	1104	Geoffrey	25	4127
Gerard	90	654	Gerard	78	653	George	21	4397
Glenn	95	591	Glenn	98	434	Gerald	49	1715
Gordon	74	977	Gordon	51	1420	Gordon	44	1973
Graeme	84	752	Graham	19	5269	Graham	22	4381
Graham	26	4377	Gregory	94	461	Harold	75	817
Gregory	78	846	Harry	100	411	Harry	65	924
Guy	85	746	Henry	83	579	Henry	63	934
Howard	92	613	Howard	68	875	Howard	64	927
Iain	94	598	Hugh	89	509	Hugh	84	666
Ian	8	12406	Ian	13	6648	Ian	23	4368
James	19	6699	James	14	6276	Ivan	91	518
Jason	93	606	Jeffrey	48	1697	Jack	81	711
Jeffrey	57	70	Jeremy	70	808	James	10	7973
Jeremy	47	1716	John	2	22290	Jeffrey	51	1519
John	5	18965	Jonathon	52	1376	John	1	32216
Jonathon	27	3985	Joseph	47	1788	Joseph	36	2313
Joseph	48	1710	Julian	96	442	Keith	14	5503
Julian	62	1371	Keith	18	5353	Kenneth	12	6130
Karl	64	1287	Kenneth	25	3287	Kevin	67	883
Keith	33	3610	Kevin	20	5051	Lawrence	83	682
Kenneth	41	1929	Lawrence	77	661	Leonard	59	1200
Kevin	15	8066	Leonard	76	663	Leslie	35	2316
Lee	50	1661	Leslie	42	2181	Malcolm	24	4156
Leslie	76	920	Malcolm	31	2836	Martin	41	2107
Malcolm	65	1247	Mark	32	2555	Maurice	62	947
Mark	4	20894	Martin	21	4425	Melvyn	78	785
Martin	18	6928	Martyn	75	677	Michael	3	20017
Martyn	87	703	Maurice	95	460	Mohammed	87	604

	1994			1984			1974	
Name	Rank	Number	Name	Rank	Number	Name	Rank	Number
Matthew	5	8593	Mohammad	83	595	Nathan	58	969
Max	72	974	Mohammed	54	1524	Neil	22	4364
Michael	12	5816	Nathan	57	1428	Nicholas	19	5183
Mitchell	77	835	Neil	42	2145	Nigel	55	1107
Mohammad	96	527	Nicholas	22	3919	Oliver	84	577
Mohammed	41	1988	Oliver	48	1808	Patrick	67	810
Nathan	27	3280	Patrick	65	930	Paul	1	15059
Nicholas	42	1900	Paul	9	7564	Peter	23	4227
Oliver	23	3786	Peter	23	3639	Philip	29	3355
Owen	99	516	Philip	32	2580	Phillip	63	895
Patrick	71	975	Phillip	64	981	Raymond	85	560
Paul	60	1289	Richard	8	7616	Richard	5	9056
Peter	51	1584	Ricky	75	712	Robert	14	6579
Philip	79	774	Robert	13	6337	Robin	75	695
Reece	54	1422	Robin	99	404	Roger	96	496
Rhys	56	1406	Ross	60	1105	Russell	60	956
Richard	49	1640	Russell	68	832	Ryan	79	614
Robert	25	3506	Ryan	28	2727	Samuel	82	596
Ross	64	1188	Sam	72	770	Scott	31	3040
Ryan	6	8327	Samuel	43	2145	Sean	56	1106
Sam	38	2148	Scott	38	2313	Shane	65	851
Samuel	9	6805	Sean	46	1875	Shaun	57	1066
Scott	37	2160	Shane	70	820	Simon	8	8333
Sean	46	1775	Shaun	52	1579	Stephen	11	7419
Shane	69	984	Simon	21	4388	Steven	17	6138
Shaun	73	974	Stephen	20	4392	Stewart	88	538
Simon	75	926	Steven	17	4805	Stuart	24	4086
Stephen	48	1661	Stewart	98	408	Terence	99	484
Steven	57	1394	Stuart	31	2613	Terry	93	513
Stuart	89	595	Terry	84	590	Thomas	40	1955
Thomas	1	11845	Thomas	11	7297	Timothy	33	2388
Timothy	76	912	Timothy	47	1874	Tony	73	734
Toby	88	607	Tony	77	648	Trevor	76	631
Tom	87	574	Wayne	50	1687	Wayne	32	2579
William	19	4238	William	34	2533	William	41	1723

	1964			1954			1944	
Name	Rank	**Number**	Name	Rank	**Number**	**Name**	Rank	**Number**
Matthew	52	1632	Michael	4	16520	Neil	80	749
Michael	6	16927	Mohamed	90	496	Nicholas	76	817
Mohammed	73	977	Mohammad	84	578	Nigel	69	873
Neil	22	5571	Mohammed	56	1231	Norman	43	2028
Nicholas	28	3908	Neil	46	1909	Patrick	31	2665
Nigel	23	4608	Nicholas	36	2431	Paul	28	3835
Patrick	35	2673	Nigel	27	3150	Peter	4	15722
Paul	2	27555	Norman	66	904	Philip	32	2656
Peter	12	10652	Patrick	39	2224	Phillip	93	514
Philip	20	5996	Paul	7	12270	Ralph	90	543
Phillip	59	1392	Peter	5	13931	Raymond	17	5212
Raymond	45	1782	Philip	16	6231	Reginald	71	864
Richard	10	11061	Phillip	57	1201	Richard	11	6719
Robert	9	11112	Raymond	26	3232	Robert	5	11315
Robin	69	1087	Richard	10	7313	Robin	57	1385
Roger	61	1374	Robert	6	12398	Rodney	48	1754
Ronald	80	833	Robin	59	1159	Roger	13	5827
Roy	71	1074	Roger	41	2186	Ronald	26	3983
Russell	55	1503	Ronald	43	2062	Roy	30	3045
Sean	36	2188	Roy	50	1597	Royston	100	421
Shaun	40	1993	Simon	53	1331	Samuel	97	450
Simon	13	8714	Stanley	86	521	Sidney	99	432
Stephen	7	15955	Stephen	3	16820	Stanley	60	1145
Steven	17	7239	Steven	23	3709	Stephen	40	2128
Stewart	83	776	Stewart	91	487	Stuart	55	1412
Stuart	32	3655	Stuart	49	1606	Terence	18	4719
Terence	51	1658	Terence	29	2885	Terry	88	599
Terry	86	709	Terry	92	487	Thomas	19	4701
Thomas	34	2726	Thomas	24	3506	Timothy	77	799
Timothy	24	4555	Timothy	40	2207	Tony	96	467
Tony	67	1216	Tony	79	646	Trevor	33	2648
Trevor	38	2072	Trevor	30	2861	Victor	56	1396
Vincent	72	1016	Victor	88	518	Vincent	94	494
Wayne	39	2030	Vincent	87	520	Walter	86	619
William	29	3840	William	15	6247	William	9	8590

3

The Top 50 names

3.1 Introduction

Did you know...

- that Henry is only to be found in the Top 50 names in the South West, and only just makes it there?
- that there are nine girls' names found in the Wales Top 50 only?
- that as many baby boys were named Oliver in East Anglia as in the South West, accounting for 1 in 66 baby boys?
- that Rebecca is at No 3 in three northern regions, but is given to more baby girls in the south, 1,683 baby girls in the South East compared with 638 babies in the East Midlands?

What were the top names in the North and how do they differ from those in the North East?

You will find the answer in the following pages, where we have looked at the Top 50 for each of the 8 standard regions of England, plus Wales. We have also subdivided the South East region into Greater London and the rest of the South East. The map opposite shows the regional and county boundaries.

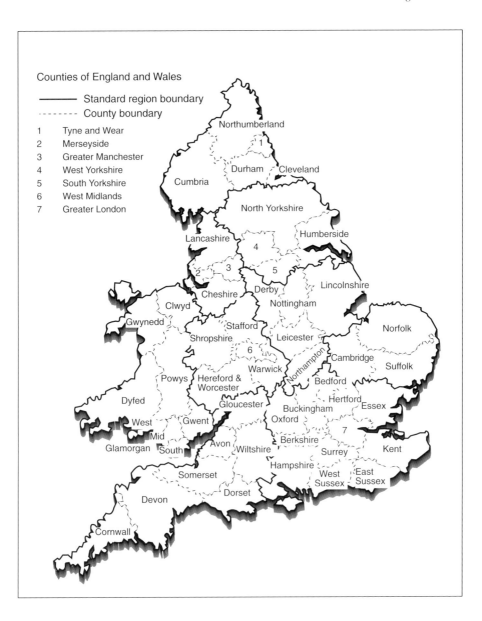

Counties of England and Wales

——————— Standard region boundary
- - - - - - - County boundary

1   Tyne and Wear
2   Merseyside
3   Greater Manchester
4   West Yorkshire
5   South Yorkshire
6   West Midlands
7   Greater London

3.2 Regional overview: Girls

The Top 50 girls' names in each region in order of rank in 1994 are shown in Tables 5–15 in sections 3.3–3.13. Frequencies are also given to enable comparisons to be made across the regions. Table D in Appendix A shows the number of NHS registrations in each region in 1994. By dividing the regional total by the frequency you can calculate the approximate number of occurrences of a selected name in the region. For example, if you want to know how many babies named Rebecca there were in the North, you look at the regional table and you will see that the name was given to 1 in 27 babies. Looking at Table D you will see that there were 17,719 baby girls in the North registered in 1994. If you divide 17,719 by 27, you get 656. So you know there were approximately 656 baby Rebeccas in the North in 1994.

The top 50 girls' names in each of the 10 regions plus Wales has been compared with the top 50 girls' names in England and Wales as a whole. Frequencies are given not only for the region, but also for England and Wales for those names in the regional listing which appear in the England and Wales Top 100. If a frequency is given of 249 or higher for girls, you know that the name is not in the England and Wales Top 50. If no frequency is given, you know that the name does not appear in the England and Wales Top 100. Whereas the differences in the choice of names between the regions in England are relatively minor, in Wales they are marked.

Difference between England and Wales

- Wales has the most names not found in the England and Wales Top 50 –13 of them.

Regional variations

- 9 of the Welsh names do not appear in other regions.
- Sara, Beth, Kate, Katherine and Abbie are not found in the top 50 anywhere but the North.
- Rosie is only in the South West Top 50.
- Leanne is only found in the West and East Midlands Top 50s.
- Only one region–the South East–has the names Jasmine, Molly and Amber.

Ranking variations

- Charlotte is least popular in Wales.
- Harriet, Alice and Georgina are ranked much higher in the south than in the north.
- Jennifer is most popular in the North West.

The number 1 spot

- Rebecca, the number 1 name in England and Wales overall, is only in the top spot in three regions–North, North West and Yorkshire and Humberside.

3.3. Girls' names in the North

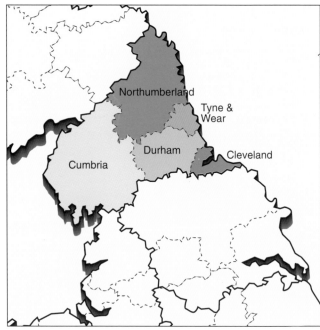

Example: Jade is joint 14th in the North, given to 1 in 70 babies in 1994. But in England and Wales it was given to 1 in 90 baby girls in 1994. You can find out its position in the England and Wales 1994 Top 100 (and the actual number of babies) using the alphabetical listing in Table 3.

Commentary

- The top 2 names in the North, Rebecca and Lauren, appear in the same position as in the England and Wales Top 50, but they are given to more baby girls in the North than the national average.

- The names Kate, Rachael and Beth in particular are given to many more baby girls in the North than in England and Wales as a whole.

- Much less popular in the North are the names Olivia and Alice.

- In the North Rebecca has the highest frequency for the top girl's name of all the regions, being given to 1 in 27 girls.

- Sarah enters the North's Top 10 at 8, displacing Emily to 13.

Table 5: Top 50 girls' names, 1994, North

Name	Rank	North 1 in	England & Wales 1 in	Name	Rank	North 1 in	England & Wales 1 in
Rebecca	1	27	40	Kate	26	130	309
Lauren	2	28	41	Rachael	27	138	342
Amy	3	36	53	Beth	28	140	403
Laura	4	39	61	Abigail	29	141	131
Jessica		39	43	Holly	30	148	129
Sophie	6	41	47	Zoe		148	150
Hannah	7	42	45	Natasha	32	150	149
Sarah	8	43	76	Alexandra	33	157	184
Emma	9	50	61	Alice	34	160	98
Charlotte	10	53	45	Kayleigh	35	163	253
Bethany	11	55	88	Melissa	36	164	201
Rachel	12	58	107	Paige		164	169
Emily	13	60	57	Elizabeth		164	143
Jade	14	70	90	Chelsea	39	167	181
Samantha		70	110	Georgia	40	169	150
Chloe	16	79	72	Shannon		169	167
Katie	17	82	84	Hayley	42	174	216
Lucy	18	94	81	Gemma	43	175	173
Danielle	19	95	113	Kirsty	44	179	182
Megan	20	96	90	Jennifer	45	181	214
Stephanie	21	97	138	Catherine		181	276
Ashleigh	22	105	272	Louise	47	183	221
Natalie	23	110	151	Abbie	48	197	330
Victoria	24	119	148	Olivia	49	199	136
Nicole	25	121	178	Anna	50	208	242

3.4. Girls' names in Yorkshire and Humberside

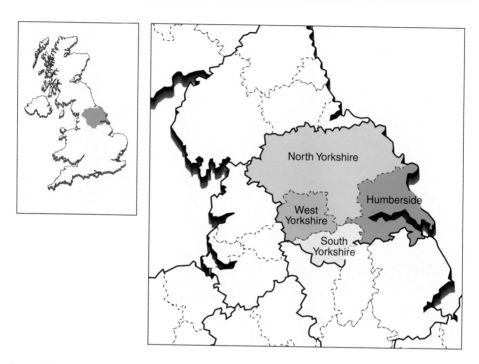

Example: Lauren is joint 1st in Yorkshire and Humberside, given to 1 in 35 baby girls in 1994. But in England and Wales it was given to 1 in 41 baby girls in 1994. You can find out its position in the England and Wales 1994 Top 100 (and the actual number of babies) using the alphabetical listing in Table 3.

Commentary

- The top 2 names in England and Wales overall, Rebecca and Lauren, appear as joint 1st in Yorkshire and Humberside, being given to 1 in 35 girls.
- Ellie is considerably more popular than in England and Wales overall, being given to 1 in 250 girls compared with 1 in 370 girls.
- Much less popular in Yorkshire and Humberside are the names Eleanor, Elizabeth, Zoe, Georgia, Alexandra and Louise.
- Bethany enters the Yorkshire Top 10 at 6, pushing Hannah out to 11.

Table 6: Top 50 girls' names, 1994, Yorkshire and Humberside

Name	Yorkshire & Humberside Rank	England & Wales 1 in	1 in	Name	Yorkshire & Humberside Rank	England & Wales 1 in	1 in
Rebecca	1	35	40	Stephanie		144	138
Lauren		35	41	Chelsea	27	148	181
Jessica	3	39	43	Kirsty	28	150	182
Charlotte	4	44	45	Melissa		150	201
Amy	5	45	53	Paige		150	169
Bethany	6	46	88	Victoria	31	151	148
Laura	7	47	61	Gemma	32	152	173
Sophie	8	48	47	Natasha	33	153	149
Emma	9	51	61	Jodie	34	154	225
Emily	10	53	57	Georgina	35	158	170
Hannah	11	54	45	Hayley	36	166	216
Chloe	12	66	72	Nicole	37	168	178
Katie	13	72	84	Shannon	38	170	167
Sarah	14	75	76	Eleanor	39	171	153
Lucy	15	79	81	Elizabeth	40	178	143
Jade	16	80	90	Kelly	41	196	261
Megan	17	82	90	Zoe	42	198	150
Danielle	18	101	113	Georgia	43	218	150
Alice	19	103	98	Alexandra	44	221	184
Olivia	20	106	136	Jennifer	45	236	214
Abigail	21	107	131	Ellie	46	250	370
Rachel	22	110	107	Harriet	47	262	268
Samantha	23	111	110	Louise	48	265	221
Natalie	24	123	151	Naomi	49	269	306
Holly	25	144	129	Amber	50	272	248

3.5 Girls' names in the East Midlands

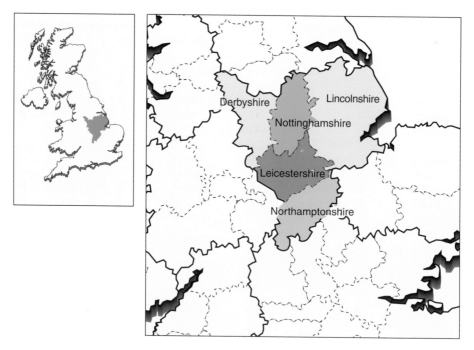

Example: Bethany is 12th in the East Midlands, given to 1 in 70 baby girls in 1994. But in England and Wales it was given to 1 in 88 baby girls in 1994. You can find out its position in the England and Wales 1994 Top 100 (and the actual number of babies) using the alphabetical listing in Table 3.

Commentary

- Lauren, 2nd in the England and Wales Top 10, takes top spot in the East Midlands Top 10, pushing Rebecca down to 3rd position.

- The names Kelly, Leanne, Nicola, Kayleigh and Harriet do not appear in the England and Wales Top 50.

- Leanne and Nicola are much more popular in the East Midlands, each being given to 1 in 233 baby girls.

- Rachel is less popular, being given to 1 in 152 girls as opposed to 1 in 107 girls in England and Wales.

Table 7: Top 50 girls' names, 1994, East Midlands

Name	Rank	East Midlands 1 in	England & Wales 1 in	Name	Rank	East Midlands 1 in	England & Wales 1 in
Lauren	1	38	41	Zoe	26	142	150
Jessica		38	43	Eleanor	27	143	153
Rebecca	3	39	40	Abigail	28	148	131
Charlotte	4	41	45	Paige	29	149	169
Sophie	5	46	47	Olivia	30	150	136
Hannah	6	47	45	Rachel	31	152	107
Emily	7	49	57	Stephanie	32	156	138
Laura		52	61	Georgina	33	157	170
Emma	9	54	61	Chelsea	34	161	181
Amy	10	56	53	Gemma	35	162	173
Chloe	11	67	72	Nicole		162	178
Bethany	12	70	88	Kirsty	37	171	182
Lucy	13	72	81	Elizabeth	38	172	143
Sarah	14	74	76	Melissa	39	174	201
Katie		74	84	Georgia	40	177	150
Megan	16	81	90	Alexandra	41	193	184
Jade	17	84	90	Jodie	42	226	225
Alice	18	93	98	Grace	43	228	235
Danielle	19	96	113	Kelly	44	233	261
Holly	20	108	129	Leanne		233	339
Samantha	21	117	110	Nicola		233	300
Natalie	22	133	151	Hayley	47	237	216
Victoria	23	135	148	Louise	48	242	221
Natasha	24	138	149	Kayleigh	49	244	253
Shannon		138	167	Harriet	50	252	268

3.6 Girls' names in East Anglia

Example: Katie is 17th in East Anglia, given to 1 in 94 baby girls in 1994. But in England and Wales it was given to 1 in 84 baby girls in 1994. You can find out its position in the England and Wales 1994 Top 100 (and the actual number of babies) using the alphabetical listing in Table 3.

Commentary

- Hannah, 5th in the England and Wales Top 10, takes pole position in East Anglia.

- There are 3 sets of jointly ranked names in the Top 10 of East Anglia – the names are more closely grouped here than in any other region.

- Jasmine does not appear in the England and Wales Top 50, but is 20th in East Anglia.

- Amber, Kayleigh, Harriet, Naomia and Francesca are much more popular in East Anglia, but Stephanie is less popular, being given to 1 in 186 baby girls compared with 1 in 130 baby girls.

- Louise is given to exactly the same number of babies, 1 in 221, as in England and Wales overall.

Table 8: Top 50 girls' names, 1994, East Anglia

Name	Rank	East Anglia 1 in	England & Wales 1 in	Name	Rank	East Anglia 1 in	England & Wales 1 in
Hannah	1	37	45	Holly		123	131
Lauren	2	38	41	VIctoria	27	126	148
Charlotte	3	39	45	Elizabeth	28	131	143
Jessica	4	42	43	Natasha	29	136	149
Rebecca	5	44	40	Danielle	30	137	113
Sophie		44	47	Gemma	31	149	173
Emily	7	49	57	Shannon		149	167
Amy	8	56	53	Georgina	33	159	170
Laura		56	61	Amber	34	163	248
Chloe	10	60	72	Kayleigh	35	168	253
Emma		60	61	Olivia		168	136
Megan	12	66	90	Chelsea	37	173	181
Lucy	13	71	81	Stephanie	38	186	138
Alice	14	74	98	Nicole	39	189	178
Bethany	15	79	88	Harriet	40	192	268
Jade	16	90	90	Alexandra	41	199	184
Katie	17	94	84	Anna	42	202	242
Sarah	18	95	76	Kirsty	43	209	182
Jasmine	19	107	252	Naomi		209	306
Georgia	20	114	150	Francesca	45	213	303
Zoe	21	116	150	Hayley	46	217	216
Rachel	22	118	107	Paige		217	169
Eleanor	23	119	153	Kelly	48	221	261
Samantha	24	122	110	Louise		221	221
Abigail	25	123	131	Molly		221	246

3.7 Girls' names in the South East including Greater London

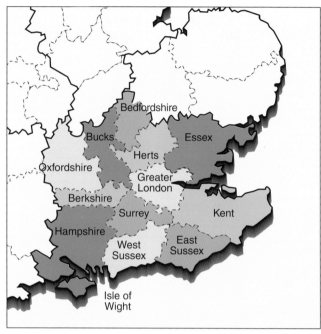

Example: Chloe is joint 10th in the whole of the South East, given to 1 in 81 babies in 1994. But in England and Wales it was given to 1 in 72 baby girls in 1994. You can find out its position in the England and Wales 1994 Top 100 (and the actual number of babies) using the alphabetical listing in Table 3.

Commentary

- Hannah takes the No 1 position in a Top 10 containing the same names as in England and Wales overall.

- Only Jasmine, Francesca and Harriet are not to be found in the England and Wales Top 50.

- Bethany is much less popular, being given to 1 in 162 baby girls as opposed to 1 in 88 baby girls in England and Wales.

- Much more popular in the whole of the South East are Francesca and Katherine.

Table 9: Top 50 girls' names, 1994, South East inc. Greater London

Name	South East, inc. G. London Rank	I in	England & Wales I in	Name	South East, inc. G. London Rank	I in	England & Wales I in
Hannah	1	47	45	Georgina	26	143	170
Charlotte	2	48	45	Stephanie	27	149	138
Rebecca	3	49	40	Abigail	28	154	131
Sophie	4	52	47	Zoe	29	158	150
Lauren		52	41	Victoria	30	161	148
Jessica	6	54	43	Bethany	31	162	88
Emily	7	60	57	Natasha	32	167	149
Amy	8	63	53	Katherine	33	173	221
Emma	9	68	61	Shannon	34	175	167
Laura	10	81	61	Paige	35	179	169
Chloe		81	72	Alexandra	36	189	184
Lucy	12	83	81	Natalie		189	151
Sarah	13	86	76	Nicole	38	198	178
Alice	14	92	98	Gemma	39	199	173
Megan	15	100	90	Louise	40	201	221
Jade	16	108	90	Anna	41	203	242
Katie	17	109	84	Grace	42	204	235
Georgia	18	120	150	Amber	43	226	248
Rachel	19	122	107	Molly	44	227	246
Holly	20	123	129	Hayley	45	232	216
Danielle	21	131	113	Jasmine	46	235	252
Olivia	22	133	136	Jennifer	47	242	214
Elizabeth	23	136	143	Francesca	48	244	303
Eleanor	24	137	153	Kirsty	49	245	182
Samantha	25	141	110	Harriet	50	250	268

3.8 Girls' names in Greater London

Example: Sophie is joint 5th in Greater London, given to 1 in 75 babies in 1994. But in England and Wales it was given to 1 in 47 baby girls in 1994. You can find out its position in the England and Wales 1994 Top 100 (and the actual number of babies) using the alphabetical listing in Table 3.

Commentary

- Jessica, Rebecca and Charlotte all tie for 2nd place in the rankings.
- Although No 1, Hannah is much less frequent, being given to 1 in 66 girls as opposed to 1 in 45.
- Far more frequently occurring in Greater London is Yasmin, being given to 1 in 293 girls compared with 1 in 537 throughout England and Wales.
- Chelsea, Melissa, Gemma and Abigail are much less popular in Greater London.
- Only Francesca, Yasmin and Ellie do not appear in the England and Wales Top 50.
- Sarah appears in the Top 10 at 8, pushing Laura out to 12.

Table 10: Top 50 girls' names, 1994, Greater London

Name	Rank	Greater London 1 in	England & Wales 1 in	Name	Rank	Greater London 1 in	England & Wales 1 in
Hannah	1	66	45	Shannon	26	196	167
Jessica	2	69	43	Nicole		196	178
Rebecca		69	40	Samantha		196	110
Charlotte		69	45	Eleanor	29	197	153
Lauren	5	75	41	Zoe	30	200	150
Sophie		75	47	Victoria	31	203	148
Amy	7	82	53	Alexandra	32	206	184
Sarah	8	87	76	Georgina	33	207	170
Emma	9	93	61	Paige	34	209	169
Emily	10	94	57	Katherine	35	210	221
Chloe	11	103	72	Grace	36	213	235
Laura	12	112	61	Natalie	37	227	151
Lucy	13	116	81	Anna	38	232	242
Georgia	14	127	150	Louise	39	238	221
Alice	15	131	98	Molly	40	251	246
Jade	16	132	90	Francesca	41	258	303
Olivia	17	140	136	Abigail	42	263	131
Rachel	18	141	107	Amber	43	280	248
Megan	19	145	90	Jennifer	44	282	214
Katie	20	157	84	Gemma	45	288	173
Elizabeth	21	158	143	Hayley		288	216
Danielle	22	159	113	Yasmin	47	293	537
Holly	23	164	129	Ellie	48	299	370
Stephanie	24	173	138	Melissa	49	308	201
Natasha	25	189	149	Chelsea	50	318	181

3.9 Girls' names in the South East excluding Greater London

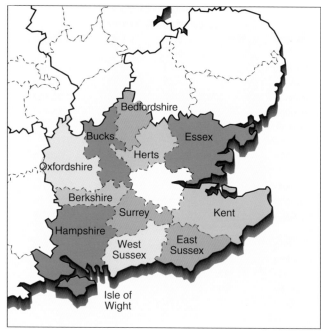

Example: Jessica is joint 6th in the South East excluding Greater London, given to 1 in 47 babies in 1994. But in England and Wales it was given to 1 in 43 baby girls in 1994. You can find out its position in the England and Wales 1994 Top 100 (and the actual number of babies) using the alphabetical listing in Table 3.

Commentary

- Charlotte and Hannah are joint 1st in a Top 10 containing exactly the same names as the England and Wales Top 10.

- Rebecca is given as frequently to babies in the region as in England and Wales overall, to 1 in 40 baby girls.

- Only Jasmine and Harriet do not appear in the England and Wales Top 50.

- Much more popular in this region is Katherine, being given to 1 in 67 girls as opposed to 1 in 221 baby girls in England and Wales overall.

- Chelsea is less popular, being given to 1 in 223 girls compared with 1 in 181.

Table 11: Top 50 girls' names, 1994, South East excl. Greater London

Name	South East, excl. G. London Rank	South East, excl. G. London 1 in	England & Wales 1 in	Name	South East, excl. G. London Rank	South East, excl. G. London 1 in	England & Wales 1 in
Charlotte	1	39	45	Abigail	26	118	131
Hannah		39	45	Elizabeth	27	124	143
Rebecca	3	40	40	Olivia	28	128	136
Sophie	4	42	47	Stephanie	29	136	138
Lauren	5	43	41	Zoe	30	137	150
Emily	6	47	57	Victoria	31	140	148
Jessica		47	43	Natasha	32	154	149
Amy	8	54	53	Katherine		154	221
Emma	9	57	61	Paige	34	162	169
Laura	10	67	61	Gemma		162	173
Lucy	11	69	81	Shannon		162	167
Chloe	12	70	72	Natalie	37	169	151
Alice	13	75	98	Alexandra	38	179	184
Megan	14	81	90	Louise	39	181	221
Sarah	15	85	76	Anna	40	186	242
Katie	16	90	84	Jasmine	41	191	252
Jade	17	95	90	Grace	42	198	235
Holly	18	104	129	Amber	43	199	248
Bethany	19	111	88	Nicole	44	200	178
Rachel	20	112	107	Harriet		200	268
Eleanor		112	153	Hayley	46	203	216
Georgia	22	115	150	Kirsty	47	210	182
Danielle	23	117	113	Molly	48	212	246
Samantha		117	110	Jennifer	49	220	214
Georgina		117	170	Chelsea	50	223	181

3.10 Girls' names in the South West

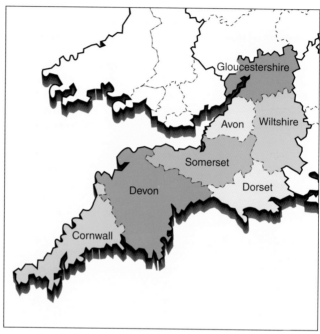

Example: Amy is 8th in the South West, given to 1 in 56 babies in 1994. But in England and Wales it was given to 1 in 53 baby girls in 1994. You can find out its position in the England and Wales 1994 Top 100 (and the actual number of babies) using the alphabetical listing in Table 3.

Commentary

- Jessica takes the top spot.
- Chloe squeezes into the Top 10, nudging Laura out.
- Much more popular in the South West are Rosie, Naomi, Harriet and Jasmine.
- Six of the names do not appear in the England and Wales Top 50.
- Out of those names which appear less frequently, the frequency of the name Sarah varies most, the name being given to 1 in 100 baby girls in the South West, compared with 1 in 76 in England and Wales overall.

Table 12: Top 50 girls' names, 1994, South West

Name	Rank	South West 1 in	England & Wales 1 in	Name	Rank	South West 1 in	England & Wales 1 in
Jessica	1	38	43	Rachel	26	128	107
Charlotte	2	39	45	Victoria	27	131	148
Sophie	3	40	47	Elizabeth	28	133	143
Hannah	4	41	45	Stephanie	29	137	138
Rebecca		41	40	Natasha	30	141	149
Lauren	6	42	41	Olivia		141	136
Emily	7	46	57	Shannon	32	144	167
Amy	8	56	53	Georgina	33	149	170
Emma	9	62	61	Jasmine		149	252
Chloe	10	64	72	Gemma	35	150	173
Laura	11	65	61	Harriet	36	153	268
Alice	12	67	98	Paige	37	160	169
Lucy		67	81	Katherine	38	166	221
Megan	14	75	90	Natalie	39	167	151
Bethany	15	76	88	Kirsty	40	172	182
Katie	16	81	84	Amber	41	184	248
Jade	17	83	90	Alexandra	42	196	184
Abigail	18	99	131	Jennifer		196	214
Sarah	19	100	76	Molly	44	203	246
Samantha	20	103	110	Chelsea	45	208	181
Holly	21	110	129	Naomi	46	209	306
Danielle	22	112	113	Kelly	47	211	261
Zoe	23	114	150	Kayleigh	48	216	253
Eleanor	24	118	153	Louise	49	219	221
Georgia	25	123	150	Rosie		219	360

3.11 Girls' names in the West Midlands

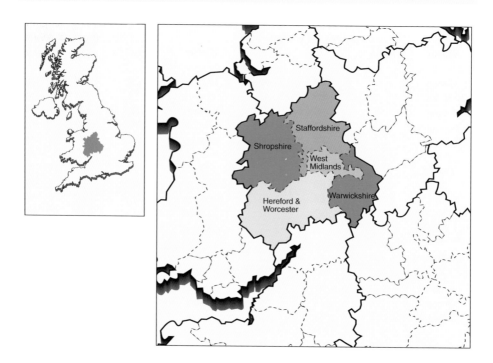

Example: Lucy is 16th in the West Midlands, given to 1 in 83 babies in 1994. But in England and Wales it was given to 1 in 81 baby girls in 1994. You can find out its position in the England and Wales 1994 Top 100 (and the actual number of babies) using the alphabetical listing in Table 3.

Commentary

* Charlotte is first in a Top 10 consisting of the same names as for England and Wales.
* Not appearing in the England and Wales Top 50 are Leanne, Kelly and Kayleigh.
* Jodie and Leanne are more popular in the West Midlands.
* Less popular are Alexandra, Georgina and Georgia.
* Sophie is given as frequently as for England and Wales, to 1 in 47 baby girls.

Table 13: Top 50 girls' names, 1994, West Midlands

Name	Rank	West Midlands 1 in	England & Wales 1 in	Name	Rank	West Midlands 1 in	England & Wales 1 in
Charlotte	1	38	45	Zoe	26	137	150
Rebecca	2	41	40	Kirsty		137	182
Jessica	3	42	43	Natalie	28	143	151
Lauren		42	41	Holly	29	144	129
Hannah	5	46	45	Jodie	30	147	225
Sophie	6	47	47	Chelsea	31	152	181
Amy	7	50	53	Victoria	32	153	148
Laura	8	52	61	Eleanor	33	155	153
Emily	9	58	57	Olivia		155	136
Emma	10	65	61	Natasha	35	160	149
Katie	11	71	84	Shannon		160	167
Chloe	12	75	72	Gemma	37	170	173
Jade	13	80	90	Hayley	38	183	216
Bethany		80	88	Melissa	39	192	201
Sarah		80	76	Nicole		192	178
Lucy	16	83	81	Grace	41	207	235
Samantha	17	96	110	Kelly	42	218	261
Danielle	18	102	113	Alexandra	43	221	184
Megan	19	103	90	Georgina	44	225	170
Alice	20	109	98	Leanne	45	238	339
Abigail	21	119	131	Louise	46	240	221
Rachel	22	123	107	Georgia	47	243	150
Elizabeth	23	127	143	Kayleigh		243	253
Paige	24	128	169	Katherine	49	254	221
Stephanie	25	131	138	Jennifer	50	256	214

3.12 Girls' names in the North West

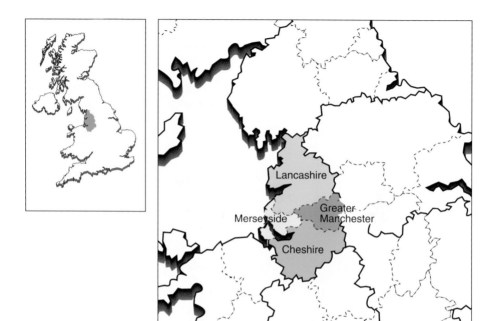

Example: Abigail is 25th in the North West, given to 1 in 121 babies in 1994. But in England and Wales it was given to 1 in 131 baby girls in 1994. You can find out its position in the England and Wales 1994 Top 100 (and the actual number of babies) using the alphabetical listing in Table 3.

Commentary

- Sarah enters the Top 10 at 10, pushing Emily out to 12.
- Not to be found in the England and Wales Top 50 are Ashleigh, Rachael, Nicola, Hayley, Leah and Heather.
- Heather is much more popular, being given to 1 in 225 baby girls in the North West as opposed to 1 in 429 babies overall.
- Less popular in the North West are the names Alice and Shannon.

Table 14: Top 50 girls' names, 1994, North West

Name	Rank	North West 1 in	England & Wales 1 in	Name	Rank	North West 1 in	England & Wales 1 in
Rebecca	1	30	40	Chelsea	26	125	181
Lauren	2	34	41	Elizabeth		125	143
Jessica	3	37	43	Natasha	28	127	149
Hannah	4	42	45	Alexandra	29	113	184
Amy	5	43	53	Alice		131	98
Sophie	6	48	47	Melissa	31	135	201
Charlotte		48	45	Holly	32	137	129
Laura	8	52	61	Victoria	33	141	148
Emma	9	54	61	Nicole	34	143	178
Sarah	10	61	76	Eleanor	35	153	153
Chloe	11	64	72	Gemma	36	160	173
Emily	12	65	57	Kirsty	37	165	182
Bethany	13	67	88	Georgia	38	173	150
Katie	14	68	84	Ashleigh	39	177	272
Rachel	15	74	107	Rachael	40	181	342
Lucy	16	76	81	Zoe	41	185	150
Megan	17	83	90	Georgina	42	191	170
Samantha	18	84	110	Paige	43	193	169
Jade	19	87	90	Nicola	44	195	300
Danielle	20	100	113	Shannon	45	203	167
Olivia		100	136	Hayley	46	205	216
Natalie	22	109	151	Leah	47	207	288
Jennifer	23	116	214	Louise	48	208	221
Stephanie	24	117	138	Heather	49	225	429
Abigail	25	121	131	Anna	50	229	242

3.13 Girls' names in Wales

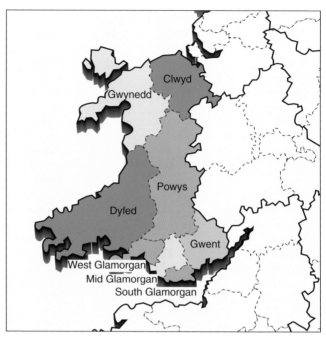

Example: Megan is 16th in the North, given to 1 in 92 babies in 1994. But in England and Wales it was given to 1 in 90 baby girls in 1994. You can find out its position in the England and Wales 1994 Top 100 (and the actual number of babies) using the alphabetical listing in Table 3.

Commentary

- Lauren takes pole position.
- Not to be found even in the England and Wales Top 100 are the names Ffion, Angharad, Lowri, Carys and Rhian.
- Not to be found in the England and Wales Top 50 are the names Stacey, Sian, Rhiannon and Bethan.
- Bethan has leapt dramatically into the Top 10 by being given to 1 in 52 Welsh baby girls as opposed to 1 in 393 babies in England and Wales overall.
- Natalie and Victoria are less popular in Wales than elsewhere.

Table 15: Top 50 girls' names, 1994, Wales

Name	Rank	Wales 1 in	England & Wales 1 in	Name	Rank	Wales 1 in	England & Wales 1 in
Lauren	1	33	41	Natasha	26	131	149
Jessica	2	35	43	Jodie	27	143	225
Hannah	3	37	45	Holly	28	146	129
Sophie	4	40	47	Stephanie	29	147	138
Rebecca	5	41	40	Gemma	30	159	173
Amy	6	50	53	Rhiannon	31	162	558
Bethan	7	52	393	Leah	32	165	288
Emily	8	53	57	Georgia	33	170	150
Charlotte	9	55	45	Angharad	34	174	
Laura	10	66	61	Chelsea		174	181
Chloe	11	68	72	Natalie	36	179	151
Emma	12	71	61	Shannon		179	167
Sarah	13	77	76	Victoria	38	181	148
Katie		77	84	Lowri	39	185	
Rachel	15	80	107	Sian	40	187	371
Megan	16	92	90	Alexandra	41	196	184
Jade	17	94	90	Carys	42	198	
Lucy	18	98	81	Kayleigh		198	253
Samantha	19	106	110	Paige		198	169
Danielle	20	111	113	Rhian		198	
Abigail	21	117	131	Kelly	46	208	261
Alice		117	98	Nicole		208	178
Zoe	23	124	150	Naomi	48	210	306
Kirsty	24	125	182	Stacey		210	387
FFion	25	126		Elizabeth	50	213	143

3.14 Regional overview: Boys

The Top 50 boys' names in each region in order of rank in 1994 are shown in Tables 16–26 in sections 3.15–3.25. Frequencies are also given to enable comparisons to be made across the regions. Table D in Appendix A shows the number of NHS registrations in each region in 1994. By dividing the regional total by the frequency you can calculate the number of occurrences of a selected name in the region. For example, if you want to know how many babies named Daniel there were in the North, you look at the regional table and you will see that the name was given to 1 in 27 babies. Looking at Table D you will see that there were 18,939 baby boys in the North registered in 1994. If you divide 18,939 by 27, you get 701. So you know there were approximately 701 baby Daniels in the North in 1994.

The top 50 boys' names in each of the 10 regions plus Wales has been compared with the top 50 boys' names in England and Wales as a whole. Frequencies are given not only for the region, but also for England and Wales for those names in the regional listing which appear in the England and Wales Top 100. If a frequency is given of 218 or higher for boys, you know that the name is not in the England and Wales Top 50. If no frequency is given, you know that the name does not appear in the England and Wales Top 100. Whereas the differences in the choice of names between the regions in England are relatively minor, in Wales they are marked.

The choice of boys' names is still surprisingly uniform. There are not many differences between the English regions and the England and Wales Top 50, but the Wales choices are markedly different.

Difference between England and Wales

- The North has the most names not found in the England and Wales Top 50 – 10 of them.

Regional variations

- Wales – all 8 of its extra names are only found in its Top 50.
- A north/south divide is seen, with Charlie, Henry, Max, George, Oliver, Harry, Nicholas, Charles and Edward only to be found in the south.

- Mohammed does not appear in Wales, East Midlands, South West, South East and East Anglia.

Ranking variations

- Samuel is markedly more unpopular in the North, ranked 28 as opposed to 5 to 14 in the rest, including 9 in the East and West Midlands.

The number 1 spot

- Thomas, the number 1 name in England and Wales overall, is number 1 in six regions excluding North, Wales, Greater London and the South East.

3.15 Boys' names in the North

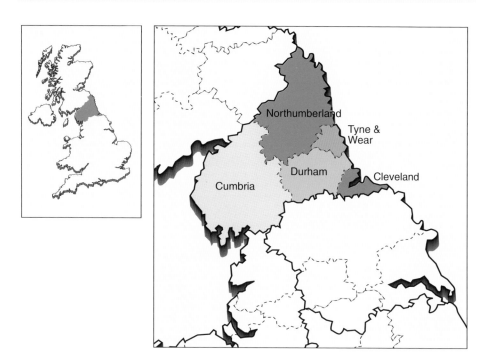

Example: Ryan is joint 2nd in the North, given to 1 in 31 babies in 1994. But in England and Wales it was given to 1 in 42 baby boys in 1994. You can find out its position in the England and Wales 1994 Top 100 (and the actual number of babies) using the alphabetical listing in Table 4.

Commentary

- Daniel, 4th in the England and Wales listings, moves into 1st place in the North.

- Adam, Michael and Liam displace Luke, Samuel and Jordan from the Top 10.

- There are 10 names which do not appear in the England and Wales Top 50.

- Much more popular in the North is Carl, given to 1 in 179 baby boys in the North compared with 1 in 500 in England and Wales overall.

- Less frequent are Samuel, William, Sean and Kyle.

Table 16: Top 50 boys' names, 1994, North

Name	Rank	North 1 in	England & Wales 1 in	Name	Rank	North 1 in	England & Wales 1 in
Daniel	1	27	33	Scott	26	90	161
James	2	31	31	Jake	27	91	79
Ryan		31	42	Samuel	28	95	51
Jack	4	33	33	Lee	29	100	244
Matthew	5	35	40	Benjamin	30	107	67
Thomas		35	29	Mark	31	118	196
Adam	7	38	59	Sam		118	161
Michael		38	60	Stephen	33	122	208
Jordan	9	40	57	Kieren	34	129	152
Liam	10	42	76	Steven	35	132	250
Andrew		42	85	Anthony	36	136	256
Chrisstopher	12	47	64	William	37	138	82
Luke	13	57	48	Sean	38	140	196
Joshua	14	60	42	Kyle	39	141	192
David	15	62	95	Aaron	40	145	133
Lewis		62	91	Craig	41	146	286
Jamie	17	73	103	Dean	42	148	323
Nathan	18	74	106	Bradley	43	149	149
Jonathan	19	75	122	Dale	44	159	286
Joseph	20	77	68	Paul		159	270
Alexander	21	80	62	Ben	46	168	169
Callum		80	125	Richard	47	169	213
Connor	23	81	118	Carl	48	179	500
Robert	24	82	99	Ross	49	188	294
John	25	86	164	Reece	50	193	244

3.16 Boys' names in Yorkshire and Humberside

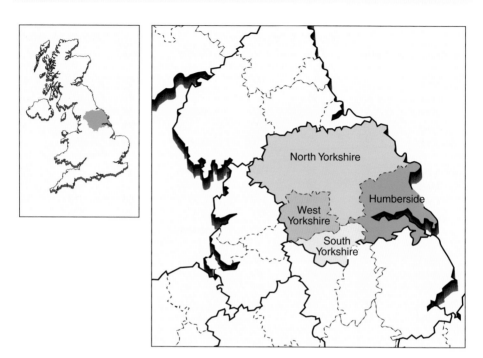

Example: Joshua is 2nd in Yorkshire and Humberside, given to 1 in 30 babies in 1994. But in England and Wales it was given to 1 in 42 baby boys in 1994. You can find out its position in the England and Wales 1994 Top 100 (and the actual number of babies) using the alphabetical listing in Table 4.

Commentary

- Thomas is 1st as in the England and Wales rankings, but Joshua moves up to 2nd from 7th and Samuel is pushed out of the Top 10 by Adam.
- Not to be found in the England and Wales Top 50 are Joe, Reece, Dale and Dominic.
- More popular in Yorkshire and Humberside is the name Dale, given to 1 in 200 baby boys compared with 1 in 286 boys overall.
- George and Harry are surprisingly less popular in Yorkshire and Humberside.
- Appearing with the same frequencies in the region as overall are James, Jack, Oliver and Andrew.

Table 17: Top 50 boys' names, 1994, Yorkshire and Humberside

Name	Yorkshire & Humberside Rank	England & Wales 1 in	1 in	Name	Yorkshire & Humberside Rank	England & Wales 1 in	1 in
Thomas	1	26	29	Bradley	26	99	149
Joshua	2	30	42	Jamie	27	100	103
James	3	31	31	Robert		100	99
Daniel	4	32	33	David	29	103	95
Jack	5	33	33	Connor	30	105	118
Matthew	6	39	40	Callum	31	115	125
Ryan	7	41	42	Jonathan		115	122
Luke	8	42	48	Jacob	33	120	152
Jordan	9	43	57	George	34	129	89
Adam	10	48	59	Kyle	35	135	192
Samuel	11	50	51	Sam	36	138	161
Joseph	12	59	68	Ben	37	139	169
Liam	13	61	76	Scott	38	146	161
Benjamin	14	63	67	John	39	153	164
Alexander	15	64	62	Kieran	40	156	152
Christopher	16	69	64	Aaron	41	160	133
Jake		69	79	Joe	42	165	244
Nathan	18	78	106	Reece	43	168	244
Lewis		78	91	Harry	44	174	123
Michael		78	60	Alex	45	178	217
Andrew	21	85	85	Dominic	46	190	238
Mohammed	22	91	175	Nicholas	47	195	182
Oliver	23	92	92	Richard	48	197	213
William	24	95	82	Dale	49	200	286
Ashley	25	97	135	Mark	50	226	196

3.17 Boys' names in the East Midlands

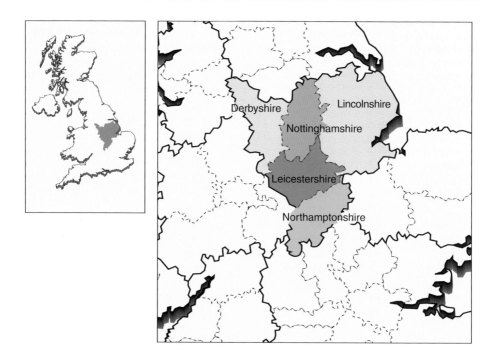

Example: Luke is 8th in the East Midlands, given to 1 in 40 babies in 1994. But in England and Wales it was given to 1 in 48 baby boys in 1994. You can find out its position in the England and Wales 1994 Top 100 (and the actual number of babies) using the alphabetical listing in Table 4.

Commentary

- The names in the Top 10 are the same as for England and Wales overall, but Adam and Jordan swop places.
- Only Joe, Reece and Dominic are not to be found in the England and Wales Top 50.
- Ashley, Alex and Kyle are much more popular in the East Midlands than in England and Wales overall.

Table 18: Top 50 boys' names, 1994, East Midlands

Name	Rank	East Midlands 1 in	England & Wales 1 in	Name	Rank	East Midlands 1 in	England & Wales 1 in
Thomas	1	26	29	Jamie	26	98	103
Jack	2	31	33	Andrew	27	99	85
Daniel	3	34	33	David	28	110	95
James		34	31	Jacob	29	113	152
Ryan	5	35	42	Connor	30	115	118
Joshua	6	36	42	Robert	31	116	99
Matthew	7	38	40	Kyle	32	125	192
Luke	8	40	48	Aaron	33	130	133
Samuel	9	43	51	Harry	34	135	123
Adam	10	54	59	Kieran	35	136	152
Jordan	11	58	57	Scott	36	145	161
Jake		58	79	Alex	37	153	217
Benjamin		58	67	Jonathan		153	122
Joseph	14	59	68	Ben	39	162	169
Alexander	15	63	62	Bradley	40	164	149
Christopher	16	68	64	John	41	172	164
William	17	69	82	Sam	42	176	161
Liam	18	70	76	Reece	43	181	244
Michael	19	76	60	Edward	44	193	208
Lewis	20	80	91	Dominic	45	208	238
Oliver	21	83	92	Mark		208	196
Ashley	22	87	135	Charles	47	210	192
George	23	91	89	Joe	48	224	244
Callum	24	94	125	Nicholas	49	224	182
Nathan	25	95	106	Peter	50	226	217

3.18 Boys' names in East Anglia

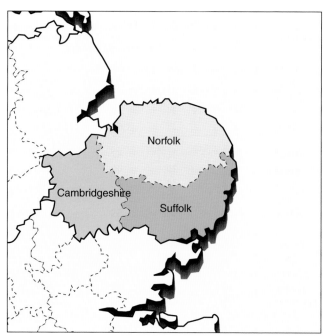

Example: Benjamin is 10th in East Anglia, given to 1 in 48 babies in 1994. But in England and Wales it was given to 1 in 67 baby boys in 1994. You can find out its position in the England and Wales 1994 Top 100 (and the actual number of babies) using the alphabetical listing in Table 4.

Commentary

- Thomas keeps pole position, but Benjamin pushes Jordan out of the Top 10.
- Dominic, Steven and Ross are not to be found in the England and Wales Top 50.
- Toby enters the Top 50, being given to 1 in 210 baby boys in East Anglia compared with 1 in 588 babies overall.
- Less popular in East Anglia is John.

Table 19: Top 50 boys' names, 1994, East Anglia

Name	Rank	East Anglia 1 in	England & Wales 1 in	Name	Rank	East Anglia 1 in	England & Wales 1 in
Thomas	1	26	29	Robert	26	100	99
James	2	27	31	Andrew	27	101	85
Jack	3	32	33	Aaron	28	106	123
Daniel	4	33	33	Harry	29	107	123
Ryan	5	35	42	Jonathan	30	121	122
Matthew	6	37	40	Kieran	31	122	152
Joshua	7	38	42	Callum	32	129	125
Luke	8	39	48	David		129	95
Samuel	9	44	51	Ben	34	132	169
Benjamin	10	48	67	Connor	35	133	118
Jordan	11	50	57	Bradley	36	141	149
Adam	12	56	59	Sam	37	147	161
Jake	13	61	79	Charles	38	162	192
Christopher	14	62	64	Edward		162	208
Alexander	15	63	62	Jacob		162	152
William	16	64	82	Scott	41	168	161
Oliver	17	66	92	Dominic	42	180	238
Lewis	18	69	91	Nicholas	43	200	182
Liam	19	70	76	Steven		200	250
Michael	20	74	60	Alex	45	203	217
George	21	75	89	Ross	46	206	294
Joseph	22	78	68	Kyle	47	210	192
Jamie	23	94	103	Toby		210	588
Nathan	24	95	106	Joe	49	213	244
Ashley	25	99	135	John		213	164

3.19 Boys' names in the South East including Greater London

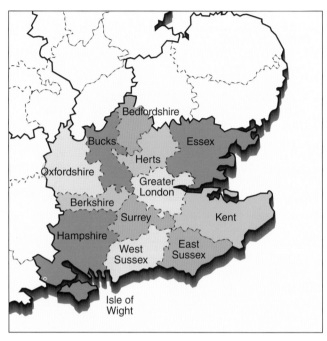

Example: Jordan is 17th in the South East, given to 1 in 73 babies in 1994. But in England and Wales it was given to 1 in 57 baby boys in 1994. You can find out its position in the England and Wales 1994 Top 100 (and the actual number of babies) using the alphabetical listing in Table 4.

Commentary

- James takes 1st place in a Top 10 which differs in composition only in that Jordan is replaced by Alexander.
- Only Charlie does not appear in the England and Wales Top 50.
- Edward, Harry and Charles are all more popular in the South East.
- Benjamin is given as frequently in the region as overall, to 1 in 67 baby boys.

Table 20: Top 50 boys' names, 1994, South East inc. Greater London

Name	South East, inc. G. London Rank	South East, inc. G. London 1 in	England & Wales 1 in	Name	South East, inc. G. London Rank	South East, inc. G. London 1 in	England & Wales 1 in
James	1	30	31	Lewis	26	106	91
Jack	2	31	33	Jamie	27	114	103
Thomas	3	32	29	Charles	28	119	192
Daniel	4	37	33	Connor	29	125	118
Matthew	5	43	40	Jonathan		125	122
Samuel	6	49	51	Aaron	31	130	133
Joshua	7	51	42	Charlie	32	140	256
Ryan	8	53	42	Sam	33	148	161
Luke		53	48	Callum		148	125
Alexander	10	54	62	Nicholas	35	150	182
Michael	11	57	60	Bradley	36	158	149
George	12	59	89	Nathan	37	159	106
Benjamin	13	67	67	Ben	38	162	169
Christopher		67	64	Edward	39	167	208
Joseph	15	69	68	Ashley	40	176	135
William	16	70	82	Jacob	41	183	152
Jordan	17	73	57	Kieran	42	187	152
Oliver	18	76	92	Mohammed		187	175
Harry	19	80	123	John	44	190	164
Adam	20	81	59	Sean	45	195	196
Jake	21	84	79	Scott	46	199	161
Robert	22	91	99	Joe	47	200	244
David	23	96	95	Stephen	48	205	208
Andrew	24	97	85	Peter	49	206	217
Liam	25	104	76	Mark	50	214	196

3.20 Boys' names in Greater London

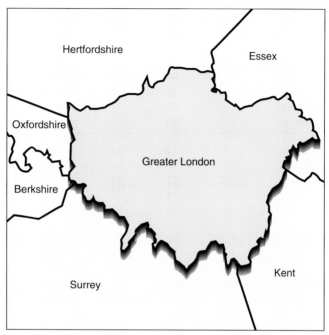

Example: Oliver is 20th in Greater London, given to 1 in 111 babies in 1994. But in England and Wales it was given to 1 in 92 baby boys in 1994. You can find out its position in the England and Wales 1994 Top 100 (and the actual number of babies) using the alphabetical listing in Table 4.

Commentary

• James is in 1st place.
• From the England and Wales Top 10 out go Joshua, Luke and Jordan, to be replaced by Michael, Alexander, and the biggest new entry, George.
• Billy is more popular in Greater London.
• Much less popular are Kieran and Callum.
• There is a much greater difference between the frequencies of the 1st and 50th names in Greater London, 1 in 40 and 1 in 275 respectively, compared with the frequencies of the 1st and 50th names in other regions.

Table 21: Top 50 boys' names, 1994, Greater London

Name	Rank	Greater London 1 in	England & Wales 1 in	Name	Rank	Greater London 1 in	England & Wales 1 in
James	1	40	31	Charlie	26	140	256
Jack	2	44	33	Andrew	27	144	85
Daniel	3	45	33	Jamie	28	157	103
Thomas	4	46	29	Aaron	29	159	133
Michael	5	64	60	Nicholas	30	162	182
Alexander	6	67	62	Jonathan	31	167	122
Matthew	7	71	40	Connor	32	179	118
Luke	8	75	48	Liam	33	184	76
Samuel		75	51	Sam		184	161
George		75	89	John	35	188	164
Joshua	11	76	42	Sean	36	189	196
Ryan	12	77	42	Lewis	37	191	91
Joseph	13	80	68	Edward	38	209	208
Christopher	14	89	64	Ben	39	213	169
Benjamin	15	99	67	Nathan	40	215	106
Harry	16	100	123	Reece	41	217	244
William	17	103	82	Anthony	42	221	256
Jordan	18	104	57	Billy		221	435
Jake	19	106	79	Bradley	44	224	149
Oliver	20	111	92	Stephen	45	229	208
Adam	21	114	59	Conor	46	232	333
David	22	115	95	Louis		232	303
Mohammed		115	175	Joe	48	241	244
Robert	24	119	99	Callum	49	243	125
Charles	25	124	192	Kieran	50	275	152

3.21 Boys' names in the South East excluding Greater London

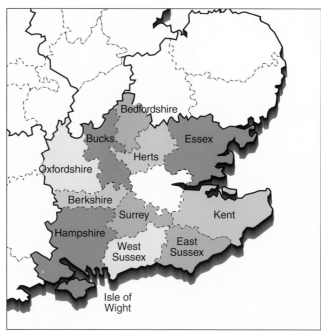

Example: Samuel is 6th in the South East excluding Greater London, given to 1 in 43 babies in 1994. But in England and Wales it was given to 1 in 51 baby boys in 1994. You can find out its position in the England and Wales 1994 Top 100 (and the actual number of babies) using the alphabetical listing in Table 4.

Commentary

- Jack is No 1 in a Top 10 where the only change in the names included is that Jordan is replaced by Alexander.
- Not to be found in the England and Wales Top 50 are Charlie, Joe and Max.
- Max is much more frequently given in the South East, to 1 in 222 babies compared with 1 in 357 in England and Wales as a whole.
- Given with the same frequency are Jamie and Andrew.

Table 22: Top 50 boys' names, 1994, South East excl. Greater London

Name	South East, excl. G. London Rank	1 in	England & Wales 1 in	Name	South East, excl. G. London Rank	1 in	England & Wales 1 in
Jack	1	27	33	David	26	93	95
James	2	28	31	Jamie	27	103	103
Thomas		28	29	Connor	28	111	118
Daniel	4	36	33	Jonathan	29	115	122
Matthew		36	40	Callum	30	124	125
Samuel	6	43	51	Aaron	31	126	133
Joshua	7	45	42	Charles	32	128	192
Ryan	8	46	42	Bradley	33	141	149
Luke	9	47	48	Sam		141	161
Alexander	10	51	62	Nathan	35	145	106
George	11	55	89	Ashley	36	149	135
Michael	12	58	60	Ben	37	150	169
Benjamin	13	59	67	Jacob	38	151	152
William	14	61	82	Charlie	39	154	256
Christopher		61	64	Nicholas	40	156	182
Jordan	16	65	57	Edward	41	158	208
Oliver	17	66	92	Kieran	42	165	152
Joseph	18	69	68	Scott	43	174	161
Adam	19	72	59	Peter	44	184	217
Harry	20	76	123	Joe	45	195	244
Jake	21	80	79	Mark	46	201	196
Robert	22	84	99	Stephen	47	207	208
Andrew	23	85	85	John	48	211	164
Liam		85	76	Sean	49	220	196
Lewis	25	86	91	Max	50	222	357

3.22 Boys' names in the South West

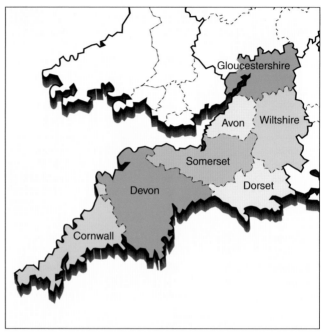

Example: Kyle is 46th in the South West, given to 1 in 203 babies in 1994. But in England and Wales it was given to 1 in 192 baby boys in 1994. You can find out its position in the England and Wales 1994 Top 100 (and the actual number of babies) using the alphabetical listing in Table 4.

Commentary

- Jack and James tie for second place in a Top 10 where the only change in composition is that Jordan is replaced by Benjamin.
- Not to be found in the England and Wales Top 50 are the names Charlie, Ross and Henry.
- Ross and Henry are far more popular in the South West than overall.
- Given with the same frequency in the South West as overall are Scott and Mark.

Table 23: Top 50 boys' names, 1994, South West

Name	Rank	South West 1 in	England & Wales 1 in	Name	Rank	South West 1 in	England & Wales 1 in
Thomas	1	26	29	Ashley	26	99	135
Jack	2	29	33	Jacob		99	152
James		29	31	Connor	28	105	118
Daniel	4	31	33	Jamie		105	103
Samuel	5	35	51	David	30	107	95
Joshua		35	42	Callum	31	109	125
Matthew	7	39	40	Aaron	32	118	133
Ryan	8	40	42	Nathan	33	121	106
Luke		44	48	Kieran	34	127	152
Benjamin	10	48	67	Bradley	35	128	149
Alexander	11	54	62	Jonathan	36	151	122
Jordan	12	56	57	Charles	37	152	192
Christopher	13	60	64	Edward	38	156	208
William	14	62	82	Scott	39	161	161
Joseph	15	63	68	Ben	40	163	169
Adam	16	64	59	Nicholas	41	164	182
Michael		64	60	Peter	42	176	217
George	18	67	89	Charlie	43	180	256
Oliver		67	92	Mark	44	196	196
Liam	20	75	76	Richard		196	213
Jake		75	79	Kyle	46	203	192
Harry	22	89	123	Sam		203	161
Lewis	23	95	91	John	48	212	164
Robert		95	99	Ross	49	217	294
Andrew	25	98	85	Henry	50	221	357

3.23 Boys' names in the West Midlands

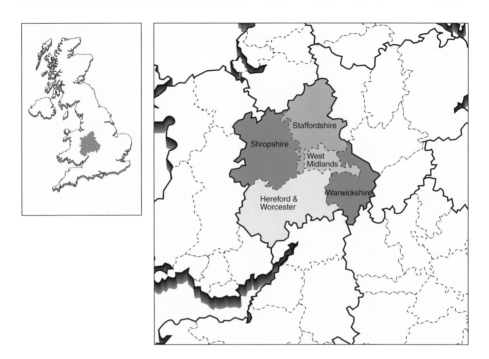

Example: Thomas is 1st in the West Midlands, given to 1 in 27 babies in 1994. But in England and Wales it was given to 1 in 29 baby boys in 1994. You can find out its position in the England and Wales 1994 Top 100 (and the actual number of babies) using the alphabetical listing in Table 4.

Commentary

- Thomas and James remain in 1st and 2nd place in a Top 10 comprising the same names as for England and Wales.
- Reece and Dale do not appear in the England and Wales Top 50.
- Dale is much higher ranked in the West Midlands, as also is Mohammed.

Table 24: Top 50 boys' names, 1994, West Midlands

Name	Rank	West Midlands 1 in	England & Wales 1 in	Name	Rank	West Midlands 1 in	England & Wales 1 in
Thomas	1	27	29	David	26	103	95
James	2	32	31	George	27	114	89
Daniel		32	33	Lewis		114	91
Jack	4	33	33	Aaron	29	116	133
Ryan	5	37	42	Robert	30	119	99
Matthew	6	39	40	Bradley	31	127	149
Luke	7	40	48	Kieran	32	129	152
Joshua	8	41	42	Connor	33	133	118
Samuel	9	52	51	Jacob	34	139	152
Jordan	10	56	57	Callum	35	142	125
Adam	11	57	59	Jonathan	36	143	122
Benjamin	12	69	67	Scott	37	156	161
Christopher	13	70	64	Harry	38	164	123
Alexander	14	71	62	Richard	39	165	213
Joseph		71	68	Alex	40	169	217
Michael	16	72	60	Ben	41	172	169
Jake	17	77	79	Kyle	42	173	192
Liam	18	79	76	Sean	43	178	196
Andrew	19	87	85	John	44	188	164
Mohammed		87	175	Sam	45	195	161
Jamie	21	91	103	Reece	46	204	244
William	22	95	82	Nicholas	47	205	182
Ashley	23	97	135	Dale	48	208	286
Nathan	24	98	106	Edward	49	214	208
Oliver	25	101	92	Mark	50	216	196

3.24 Boys' names in the North West

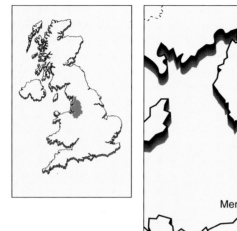
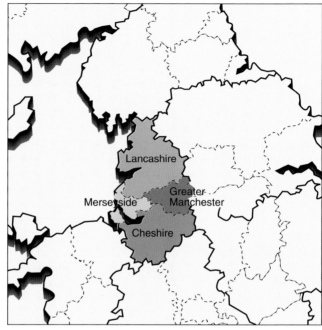

Example: Ryan is 6th in the North West, given to 1 in 34 babies in 1994. But in England and Wales it was given to 1 in 42 baby boys in 1994. You can find out its position in the England and Wales 1994 Top 100 (and the actual number of babies) using the alphabetical listing in Table 4.

Commentary

- Adam, Michael and Liam displace Luke, Samuel and Jordan from the England and Wales Top 10.
- Not to be found in the England and Wales Top 50 are Anthony, Paul, Lee and Dominic.
- Much more frequently given are the names Alexander, Anthony, Paul and Lee.
- Ashley and George are not given as frequently as in England and Wales overall.
- James is given as frequently in the North West as overall, to 1 in 31 babies.

Table 25: Top 50 boys' names, 1994, North West

Name	Rank	North West 1 in	England & Wales 1 in	Name	Rank	North West 1 in	England & Wales 1 in
Thomas	1	27	29	Callum	26	111	125
Daniel	2	28	33	John	27	112	164
James	3	31	31	Connor	28	113	118
Jack	4	32	33	Mohammed		113	175
Matthew	5	33	40	Sean	30	117	196
Ryan	6	34	42	William	31	118	82
Joshua	7	41	42	Oliver	32	119	92
Adam		41	59	Kieran	33	135	152
Michael	9	43	60	Mark	34	139	196
Christopher	10	52	64	Bradley	35	143	149
Jordan		52	57	Kyle	36	146	192
Joseph	12	54	68	Aaron	37	148	133
Luke	13	55	48	Anthony	38	150	256
Samuel	14	57	51	Jacob	39	154	152
Liam	15	60	76	Paul	40	157	270
Alexander	16	64	62	Scott	41	158	161
Andrew		64	85	Stephen		158	208
Benjamin	18	74	67	George	43	161	89
Lewis		74	91	Sam	44	162	161
Jake		74	79	Lee	45	172	244
Nathan	21	90	106	Ashley	46	183	135
Robert	22	91	99	Ben	47	187	169
David	23	92	95	Peter	48	191	217
Jonathan	24	98	122	Richard	49	196	213
Jamie	25	108	103	Dominic	50	197	238

3.25 Boys' names in Wales

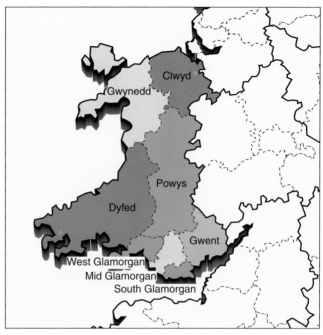

Example: Aaron is 35th in Wales, given to 1 in 138 babies in 1994. But in England and Wales it was given to 1 in 133 baby boys in 1994. You can find out its position in the England and Wales 1994 Top 100 (and the actual number of babies) using the alphabetical listing in Table 3.

Commentary

- Daniel takes the top spot in a Top 10 where the only change in composition is that Samuel is pushed out by Rhys.
- There are 5 names not to be found in the England and Wales Top 100.
- Gareth, Owen and Rhys do not appear in the England and Wales Top 50.
- Much less popular in Wales is the name Oliver.
- Thomas is given as frequently in Wales as overall, to 1 in 29 of the baby boys.

Table 26: Top 50 boys' names, 1994, Wales

Name	Rank	Wales 1 in	England & Wales 1 in	Name	Rank	Wales 1 in	England & Wales 1 in
Daniel	1	27	33	Andrew	26	102	85
Thomas	2	29	29	Ashley	27	105	135
Joshua	3	30	42	Robert	28	110	99
James	4	33	31	Scott	29	112	161
Ryan	5	36	42	Kyle	30	113	192
Jack	6	43	33	Callum	31	118	125
Jordan	7	44	57	Gareth	32	124	588
Luke	8	46	48	Connor		124	118
Matthew	9	49	40	Kieran	34	133	152
Rhys	10	55	250	Aaron	35	138	133
Nathan	11	56	106	Jacob	36	139	152
Adam	12	57	59	Alex	37	154	217
Samuel		57	51	Richard	38	159	213
Liam	14	59	76	Ieuan	39	164	
David		59	95	Oliver	40	172	92
Michael	16	67	60	Lloyd	41	179	
Christopher	17	72	64	Sean	42	180	196
Alexander	18	78	62	John	43	188	164
Benjamin		78	67	Sam		188	161
Lewis	20	79	91	Owen	45	190	667
Joseph	21	82	68	Nicholas	46	199	182
Jamie	22	93	103	Ben	47	213	169
Jake	23	94	79	Aled	48	224	
Jonathan		94	122	Tomos		224	
William	25	100	82	Sion	50	227	

4

Further information

4.1 Birth, Death and Marriage Certificate Services from the GRO

The General Register Office (GRO) maintains records of births, deaths and marriages registered in England and Wales since 1 July 1837 and certain records of births, deaths and marriages which occurred abroad. Each year GRO processes almost half a million applications for certificates, which are essential source documents not only for genealogists, family historians and researchers but also for proving age and entitlement when applying for passports, benefits etc.

Certificate application services

By post
For an application form and list of fees, write to: General Register Office, PO Box 2, Merseyside PR8 2JD.

In person
You can search the Indexes to the records yourself and make your application in person at the Public Search Room (PSR), St Catherine's House, 10 Kingsway, London WC2B 6JP. The PSR is open between 08.30 and 16.30 Monday to Friday.

By telephone
Telephone 0151 471 4524 to order your certificates using credit or debit cards.

Priority service
If you need your certificate urgently, you can order it either in person or by telephone (see above) for delivery on the next working day at a higher fee.

Commemorative certificates
For a special certificate to commemorate a Golden or Diamond Wedding anniversary, telephone 0151 471 4256.

Appendix A

How the lists were compiled

This booklet has been compiled from names of people on the National Health Service Central Register, which is a central register of all people in England and Wales who are registered with a general practitioner (GP). This register was computerised in 1991. OPCS has counted the number of people on the register born in the selected years given in this booklet, as shown in Table C.

For the years of birth prior to 1994, the names on the register are not exactly the same as the names of people born in those years in England and Wales. This is because the register includes people who came into the country from abroad and registered with a general practitioner. Also, it excludes people who died or who left the country to live abroad prior to 1991.

The names on the register are those in current use. These are not always the same as those given at birth registration.

These differences will have a relatively small impact on the distribution of names. The most obvious exception is Mohammed and similar variations, where, starting with people born in 1954, these are increasingly popular. This reflects the effects of immigration rather than naming practice in England and Wales at that time. Increasingly, inclusion of these names in more recent lists is a genuine reflection of naming of babies born in this country. For 1994 virtually all the babies named Mohammed would have been born in this country.

For 1994, OPCS has counted the number of babies in the regions who were registered with a general practioner in each of the regions, as shown in Table D. Not all the babies born in that year on the NHSCR would have been registered with a general practitioner by the end of the year.

Table C – NHS Registrations by sex and year of birth

Year	Males	Females	Persons
1944	382,217	373,377	755,594
1954	394,627	387,138	781,765
1964	504,911	502,850	1,007,761
1974	357,274	350,305	707,579
1984	347,467	331,682	679,149
1994	347,986	329,739	677,725

Table D – NHS Registrations by sex, births in 1994, Standard Regions

Region	Males	Females	Persons
North	18,939	17,719	36,658
Yorkshire & Humberside	32,040	30,710	62,750
East Midlands	26,010	24,905	50,915
East Anglia	12,792	11,934	24,726
South East	122,682	116,226	238,908
Greater London	51,097	48,714	99,811
Rest of South	71,585	67,512	139,097
South West	28,448	26,997	55,445
West Midlands	34,717	33,082	67,799
North West	41,345	38,987	80,332
Wales	17,672	17,036	34,708
England & Wales	334,645	317,596	652,241

7